desserts
new healthy kitchen

RECIPES

Annabel Langbein

GENERAL EDITOR

Chuck Williams

PHOTOGRAPHY

Dan Goldberg & Ben Dearnley

BONNIER
BOOKS

contents

About this book

The books in the New Healthy Kitchen series offer simple and appealing ways to enjoy a diet rich in fruits, vegetables, and grains.

We are blessed with an abundance of food, from superb raw ingredients to highly processed convenience foods, but it's easy to get stuck in a food rut or make unhealthy choices. Since the foods you eat directly affect your overall health and your energy level, incorporating a wide selection of fresh produce and whole grains into your diet and cooking food yourself are two of the best things you can do to eat both healthfully and well.

The recipes in *Desserts* are organised in a new way: by the colour of the fruits and vegetables used in the dishes. A chapter on wholegrains, nuts, and seeds rounds out the book with appealing ways to enjoy such supremely wholesome foods. This accessible and informative approach shows how each colour group contributes different benefits to your health. Thinking about the colour of foods is an easy way to make sure you're consuming all the fresh produce you need. If you remember to eat at least one fruit or vegetable from each colour group daily, as part of a meal, as a snack, and for dessert, you are well on your way to enjoying a varied and nutritious diet.

The New Healthy Kitchen series will bring colour and creativity into your kitchen while helping you to use a wide variety of fresh produce and whole grains in your meals every day.

Eating the rainbow

Purple and blue fruits and vegetables contain fibre, vitamins, and phytochemicals that promote heart health; help memory function; lower the risk of some cancers; promote urinary tract health; and boost immunity

White and tan fruits and vegetables contain fibre, vitamins, and phytochemicals that promote heart health; help maintain healthful cholesterol levels; lower the risk of breast, lung, and other cancers; and slow cholesterol absorption

Green fruits and vegetables contain fibre, vitamins, and phytochemicals that lower the risk of breast, prostate, lung, and other cancers; promote eye health; help build strong bones and teeth; and boost immunity

Red fruits and vegetables contain fibre, vitamins, and phytochemicals that promote heart health; help memory function; lower the risk of some cancers; promote urinary tract health; and boost immunity

Brown whole grains, pulses, seeds, and nuts include fibre, vitamins, and phytonutrients that lower blood cholesterol levels and reduce the risk of colon and other cancers, diabetes, heart disease, and stroke

Yellow and orange fruits and vegetables contain fibre, vitamins, and phytochemicals that promote heart health; promote eye health; lower the risk of some cancers; and boost immunity

Adapted from educational materials of the Produce for Better Health Foundation

The new healthy kitchen

Popular diet regimes often focus on forbidding or restricting certain foods. Cut out all fat. Avoid carbs. Eat lots of grapefruit, or nothing but cabbage soup. Despite the promises of such fads, nutritionists are growing ever more certain that what we truly need for optimum health is variety. Our bodies require a number of essential nutrients and the best way to get them is to eat a wide range of fresh foods.

The New Healthy Kitchen series takes the approach that healthy food is good, fresh food, simply prepared to bring out its appealing flavours and beautifully presented to delight the senses. For desserts, this means starting with high-quality ingredients, especially fresh fruits, a variety of nuts, dark chocolate, and the occasional whole grain, and preparing them with an eye to preserving their inherent colours and textures as well as their valuable nutrients. The recipes in this healthy cookbook emphasize freshness, colour, flavour, and variety.

Our bodies need the vitamins, minerals and fibre provided by a wide range of plant foods in order to stay healthy. In addition to supplying these essentials, fruits, vegetables, and grains are also rich in phytochemicals, beneficial compounds found only in plants. In many cases, the phytochemicals are what give fruits and vegetables their vibrant colours and distinctive flavours. They also help our bodies fight off disease and damage.

Unfortunately, our modern diet is remarkably limited in the kind of plant foods we eat. With the abundance of all types of food at our disposal, we tend to over-indulge in concentrated sources of energy, especially animal fats. We also gravitate towards carbohydrates, which are excellent sources of quick energy; however, some common carbohydrates, such as refined flours, are stripped of the wholesome nutrients found in whole grains.

Popping pills and taking supplements aren't the best solutions to a lack of vitamins and minerals in the diet. Allowing your body to extract these nutrients from different foods is the very best way of getting what you need, in the natural form in which your body is designed to use it.

Current nutritional guidelines recommend eating at least four servings of fruit each day, plus five servings of vegetables. A serving is not large, but to ensure that you get a wide range of nutrients, you should vary the fruits and vegetables you eat. This cookery book offers many delicious ways to include fruit

in your meals each day. Additionally, a good portion of the food you eat daily should come from grains, nuts, and seeds. These foods are rich in fibre, protein, and minerals. While whole grains play only a small role in sweet dishes, it's hard to imagine desserts without nuts and two other favourite seeds: the coffee bean and the cocoa bean.

Paying attention to the colour of ingredients when you prepare desserts will help you remember to bring a wide variety of bright, ripe produce into your diet. Keeping the focus on colour also increases the benefits to your health, since each colour of fruit, from red cherries to green grapes to yellow lemons, provides different health-enhancing phyto-chemicals. To help you enjoy all the wonderful plant foods that can play a role in an after-

dinner treat, the chapters in this book are organised by the five prominent colour groups of fresh foods: purple and blue, green, white and tan, yellow and orange, and red. A sixth chapter focuses on the "brown" ingredients: whole grains, nuts, and seeds, including coffee and chocolate.

Each chapter begins with a chart showing which fruits are at their peak of ripeness each season. The Brown chapter chart shows which grains, pulses, nuts, and seeds might figure in a delicious dessert. The recipes themselves are simple and straight-forward, designed for real-life cooks who haven't much time to spare, but want to use what time they do have to prepare healthy, colourful, and above all delicious foods for themselves and their families.

Fruits & vegetables

Fresh produce is one of the foundations of a healthy diet. Fruits, in particular, are some of the most beautiful foods on earth – a gift to all the senses, with vibrant colours, heady perfumes, and flavours that range from tart to sweet. Many fruits are appealing enough to serve as a treat when simply eaten in the hand, and the sweetness inherent in some vegetables can make for a wonderful dessert.

In the early years of the twentieth century, researchers discovered that fruits and vegetables contain the various vitamins and minerals we now know are essential to maintaining good health and fighting disease. We are entering into a similarly exciting era of discovery, as we learn about the roles that phytochemicals play in our bodies.

These protective compounds found in plants, believed to number in the thousands, work alone and in combination with one another and with nutrients. They work in different ways. For example, some phytochemicals act as antioxidants, which protect the body by neutralising unstable oxygen molecules (known as free radicals) that damage cells and promote disease. Eating plant foods rich in antioxidants can reduce the incidence of various cancers, heart disease, impaired vision, and other health problems. Fruits and vegetables from each of the colour groups provide us with their own unique combination of phytonutrients, each playing its own role in fighting disease and promoting health.

By eating a wide variety of fruits and vegetables at their peak of ripeness, you will not only please your palate, but you will also give your body the benefit of all the healthy nutrients that these foods contain.

Grains & seeds

Grains, which are the seeds of plants, contain a wealth of nutrients. They are rich in vitamins and minerals, protein, and fibre, all of which are essential to a healthful diet. Whole grains don't make many appearances at dessert time, but they should not be discounted altogether. For the sweet purposes of this book, they can be grouped with a few other beneficial seeds: nuts, coffee, and chocolate.

Like vegetables and fruits, grains contain beneficial phytochemicals in addition to a number of essential nutrients. When a grain is refined – as when wheat is made into white flour – the fibre-rich hull and the nutrient-rich germ are removed, leaving the endosperm, which is largely starch. Although white flour and other refined grains are often enriched with a few nutrients that have been removed in milling, important components such as fibre and phytochemicals are not replaced. As a result, eating refined grains, as well as refined sugars, raises the blood sugar level and upsets the body's balance. By contrast, eating whole grains can help maintain healthful cholesterol levels.

Nuts, another type of plant seed, are rich in omega-3 fatty acids, substances that are essential to brain function and also good for the heart. Nuts are also loaded with fibre, which helps maintain low cholesterol levels, and with vitamin E, an antioxidant linked to decreased risk of heart disease.

Two other seed-based foods, coffee and chocolate, are of special interest in a dessert cookbook. They may not seem like health foods, but both offer a number of valuable health benefits. Coffee is packed with antioxidants, as well as minerals such as magnesium. Cocoa beans, a primary ingredient in chocolate, contain more than six hundred plant chemicals, including anti-

oxidants such as catechins, which are also found in fruits, vegetables, and red wine. The darker the chocolate, the better; milk chocolate has a lower percentage of chocolate liquor from cocoa beans and more added sugar as well as milk.

The Brown chapter celebrates the virtues of eating desserts made with coffee and dark chocolate. It also provides delicious ways to enjoy whole grains and several varieties of nuts. White flour is usually the grain of choice for desserts, but whole grains can make desserts more interesting and filling. Combining these foods with fruits will make the finale of your meal as satisfying and appealing as the main course.

Other ingredients

The New Healthy Kitchen philosophy is to eat a wide variety of wholesome foods, rather than to limit what you eat. The mainstays of your diet should be fruits and vegetables, with an emphasis on whole grains and pulses as well. While fat and sugar should make up just a small percentage of the food you eat, they are essential in many desserts. Enjoying them in moderation is the key.

The flavour and texture of a pastry crust is not the same without sweet butter, and cheese makes a delicious partner for many fruits. Even when a dessert is somewhat rich, it is more wholesome if you prepare it yourself using high-quality, fresh ingredients rather than serving sweets from a packet that contain artificial additives and preservatives. Some of the desserts in *Desserts* are luxurious (nutritional analyses on pages 130–33

will help you determine how rich a particular dessert is). In such cases, keep in mind that a little goes a long way. Enjoy a rich treat, but cut slender slices and save leftovers for another day instead of offering second helpings. Even for desserts made with fruits and other healthy ingredients, a serving is not as generous as you may think. When you know that dessert is on the day's menu, eat a lighter lunch or dinner than you normally

would. The desserts in *Desserts* include dairy foods in the form of milk and cream, cheese, yoghurt, sour cream, crème fraîche, and butter. When choosing these ingredients, especially milk and yoghurt, look for organics, as they have the best flavour. Skimmed milk, low-fat yoghurt, and light sour cream can be used in most desserts if the whole versions are too heavy for you. (If best flavour and texture is your main concern, try full-cream dairy foods.) Non-fat and low-fat dairy foods will not work as well in most cakes and other baked goods. Always choose unsalted butter for fresher flavour and so that you can control the amount of salt in your cooking.

Eggs play another essential role in making desserts. Depending on how they are treated, they can help create the airy texture of a soufflé or meringue, the smooth richness of a flan or ice cream, or the moist crumb of a cake. A few years ago, eggs were regarded with suspicion from a health standpoint because of their cholesterol content, but this view has shifted as researchers learn more about how the body processes cholesterol. Eggs are now considered a highly nutritious part of a healthy diet, and eating eggs may even reduce the risk of heart disease and stroke, among other benefits.

While uncooked fruits at their seasonal peak need minimal sweetening, cooked fruit desserts regularly call for some kind of sweetener. Whenever possible, use unrefined sweeteners such as maple syrup and unfiltered honey. Both make a particularly good glaze for grilled fruits. Well-flavoured honeys, such as wildflower or lavender, can transform a bowl of perfectly ripe fresh fruit and natural yoghurt into an after-dinner treat. In recipes that call for sugar, you can use organic granulated sugar or icing sugar. Turbinado sugar, raw sugar that has been cleaned by steaming, has a coarse texture and tan colour that make it a delightful condiment sprinkled over sliced raw fruit.

Acidic ingredients can bring out a fruit's flavour without making a dessert heavy. Add a little lemon juice and/or lemon zest to almost any cooked fruit dessert, from an apple crisp to a winter fruit compote, and taste to see how it intensifies the fruit's flavour. Even vinegars boost the taste of fruits; try raspberry vinegar with sugar on peaches, or the classic Italian combination of aged balsamic vinegar and freshly ground black pepper sprinkled over ripe strawberries (page 101).

Liqueurs, wine, and some spirits such as rum also complement and intensify the flavour of many fruits – and red wine in particular contributes heart-healthy phyto-nutrients. Many spices marry beautifully with fruit, especially cinnamon, nutmeg, cardamom, and mace. While mint is a classic garnish for fruit, other fresh herbs, such as lavender, basil, thyme, and rosemary, give fruit desserts an ineffable, unique taste.

Creating the healthy dessert

Cooking at home is the best way to ensure that your food tastes good, retains as many nutrients as possible, and doesn't include additives you don't need. But the time it takes to plan, shop for, and prepare home-made meals is increasingly scarce as our lives become ever more complex. Luckily, the New Healthy Kitchen is designed for real-life cooks with real-life schedules.

Each recipe begins by noting the amount of time needed to prepare and cook it, so you can better plan the time it takes to create a homemade dessert. The "Fresh Ideas" in each chapter describe simple after-dinner dishes that are easier to make than going out to buy similar prepared desserts. During your busy day, you may be able to snack on

colourful fresh and dried fruits, but the evening meal is a good opportunity to use the recipes in *Desserts,* which allow you to include foods from all the colour groups in the healthy-eating rainbow. You can plan your meals not just by what is available in the shops, but also by the colour of the main ingredient in each course. When combined,

the courses will make a colourful menu from starter to dessert. Your plates and table will be colourful, and your menu healthy.

Fruit is the perfect dessert to follow any recipe in the *Main Dishes* book of the New Healthy Kitchen series. Whether whole and raw or cooked into an elegant tart, fruit aids the digestion and doesn't overwhelm the palate or overfill the stomach. Just as you balance colours by including a range in your menu, you can balance strong flavours with mild ones. Fruit desserts are the perfect finale to a meaty main course, as their sweetness complements beef, pork, and lamb, as well as rich duck. A fruit sorbet is an ideal follow-up to a spicy main dish. Citrus-based desserts such as Silky Lime Mousse (page 42) and Lemon Soufflés (page 86), are particularly good after a meal that includes fish.

The desserts in the New Healthy Kitchen range from grilled pineapple glazed with honey and flavoured with star anise (page 76) to elegant lavender-infused flans garnished with plums (page 24). Among the baked sweets are Blackberry Crumble (page 23),

Walnut & Date Tart (page 124), and Oatmeal Pear Crisp (page 123). While most of the desserts in *Desserts* are fruit-based, vegetables make an appearance too – in Carrot Cupcakes (page 82) and Chocolate-Pumpkin Cake (page 120). Grains such as oats and cornmeal are used in toppings and crusts.

As the recipes in *Desserts* make clear, eating healthily is not about sacrifice or denial, but about moderation. Small amounts of added sweeteners intensify the natural sweetness of fruits, vegetables, and nuts, while a little butter rounds out the taste of a dessert and makes it more satisfying.

The preparation and cooking techniques used in *Desserts* range from simply cutting up and seasoning fresh fruit to making

easy mousses and sorbets. The glossary in the back of the book lists all the fresh ingredients used in the recipes and provides information on how to judge ripeness, where to source the ingredients and how to store fruit when you bring it home.

Finally, when you don't have the time or inclination to make a dessert, take a hint from the cuisines of the Near East, Southeast Asia, and the Mediterranean, and serve whole fruit. Nature, with the help of plant breeders and growers, has already done most of the work for you, creating beautifully coloured and uniquely shaped foods for you to enjoy. Savouring the pure taste of fresh fruit is a delicious, healthy, and fitting end to any healthy meal.

purple figs dried currants

raisins blackberries blue grapes

blue plums fresh blackcurrants

prunes lavender purple grapes

blueberries black plums purple

figs raisins dried currants

Purple & blue

For many people – especially nutritional scientists – purple and blue are favourite colours. The list of fruits in this group is short, but they constitute some of the most luscious and appealing produce available. They are also among the richest in disease-fighting antioxidants. Blueberries, in particular, have been studied extensively for their ability to improve memory and brain function.

Blackberries, which share many of the characteristics of blueberries, grow wild on brambles all over the country, just waiting for you to harvest them in early autumn. Use them to make a simple crumble (page 23).

Ripe summer plums are prized by the French, especially the purple-black prune plum used to make the dried version. Plums are packed with nutrients as well as fibre. In the summertime, try ending a meal with simple and delicious baked plums (page 28).

You might think of purple grapes as a treat more than a health food, but grapes contain many of the same heart-healthy compounds as red wine. Use purple grapes to make an elegant tart (page 34).

Lavender flowers are edible and delicious, and have a phytochemical profile similar to that of blue fruits. Flavouring a simple custard with lavender (page 24) is a unique way to add a new blue ingredient to your puddings. Many blue fruits are at their best in the warm months, but even in mid-winter, you can enjoy them in their dried forms.

SPRING	SUMMER	AUTUMN	WINTER
blueberries	blackberries	blueberries	currants
currants	blueberries	blackcurrants	blue, purple, or black grapes
blue, purple, or black grapes	blackcurrants	purple figs	prunes
blue, purple, or black plums	purple figs	blue, purple, or black grapes	raisins
prunes	blue, purple, or black grapes	blue, purple, or black plums	
raisins	lavender	prunes	
	blue, purple, or black plums	raisins	
	prunes		
	raisins		

blackberry crumble

4 apples

1 lb (450 g) fresh or frozen blackberries

2 tsp cornflour

125 g (4 oz) granulated sugar

125 g (4 oz) plain flour

185 g (6 oz) demerera sugar

90 g (1 cup/3 oz) rolled oats

60 g (2 oz) dessicated coconut

75 g (2½ oz) chopped almonds

2 tsp ground cinnamon

½ tsp ground ginger

125 g (4 oz) butter, melted

Preheat oven to165°C (325°F). Peel, core, and thinly slice the apples.

Stir berries, apples, cornflour, and granulated sugar together in a bowl, then spread in a baking dish 30–35 cm (12–14 inches) in diameter.

Stir flour, demerera sugar, oats, coconut, almonds, cinnamon, and ginger together in a bowl. Drizzle with melted butter and toss with a fork to combine. Sprinkle evenly over fruit. Bake until golden and crisp, 45–50 minutes. Serve warm.

Notes: Apples will remain somewhat firm after crumble is baked. If you prefer softer apples, cook them in a covered microwave-proof dish for 7 minutes before mixing with berries. The crumble mixture can be made in bulk to have on hand for quick baked fruit desserts. It will keep in refrigerator for 4 weeks, or can be frozen for longer storage.

To prepare: 20 minutes

To cook: 45–50 minutes

6–8 servings

raisin & cashew truffles

185 g (6 oz) raisins

185 g (6 oz) currants

185 g (6 oz) Brazil nuts

185 g (6 oz) unsalted roasted cashew nuts

185 g (6 oz) dessicated coconut

3 Tbsp chopped crystallised ginger

2 Tbsp sweetened condensed milk

Using a food processor or chef's knife, finely chop and blend raisins, currants, Brazil nuts, cashew nuts, 125 g (4 oz) coconut, and the ginger. Transfer to a bowl, combine with condensed milk, and stir to blend into a paste. Shape into small balls. Spread remaining 60 g (2 oz) coconut on a plate and roll truffles in coconut to coat. Serve at once, or store in an airtight container in refrigerator for up to 4 weeks.

To prepare: 30 minutes

About 50 small truffles

lavender flans

125 g (4 oz) plus 3 Tbsp sugar

1 l (1¾ pints) low-fat or full-cream milk

10 stems organic fresh lavender, tied in a bunch

5 eggs

1 tsp pure vanilla extract

2 or 3 fresh purple plums, stoned and diced, or 60 g (2 oz) fresh whole blueberries

Preheat oven to 165°C (325°F). Combine 125 g (4 oz) sugar and 2 Tbsp water in a small saucepan, swirling the pan over medium-high heat until mixture turns a rich amber colour, about 9 minutes. While sugar cooks into a caramel, occasionally brush around inner rim of pan with a wet pastry brush to prevent syrup from crystallising on pan sides. Remove caramel from heat and divide among eight 180–250-ml (6– to 8–fl oz) ramekins or custard cups.

Combine milk with 3 Tbsp sugar and lavender in a saucepan. Bring to a simmer over medium heat, stirring until sugar has dissolved, then remove from heat. Let stand for 15 minutes, then discard lavender.

Lightly whisk eggs and vanilla together in a bowl until just combined (do not overbeat). Stir into warm milk. Strain mixture into prepared ramekins. Place ramekins in a deep baking dish. Pour hot water into dish to come halfway up sides of ramekins. Bake until flans are set, about 35 minutes. Remove from water bath and leave to cool. Cover and chill for at least 8 hours or up to 2 days to infuse flans with caramel flavour.

Remove flans from refrigerator 30 minutes before serving. Slide a knife around edge to loosen each flan and turn out onto a serving plate. Caramel sauce will pour out on to plates. Scatter diced plums or berries around flans and serve.

To prepare: 20 minutes

To cook: 45–50 minutes, plus at least 8 hours to chill

8 servings

blueberry cake with crunchy walnut topping

Crunchy Walnut Topping

60 g (2 oz) **walnut or pecan pieces**

60 g (2 oz) **brown sugar**

2 Tbsp **plain flour**

1 tsp **ground cinnamon**

2 Tbsp **butter, melted**

Cake

125 g (4 oz) **butter, softened**

155 g (5 oz) **granulated sugar**

1 **egg at room temperature**

1 tsp **pure vanilla extract**

125 ml (4 fl oz) **low-fat sour cream**

280 g (9 oz) **plain flour**

2 tsp **baking powder**

½ tsp **bicarbonate of soda**

125 g (4 oz) **fresh or frozen blueberries or raspberries**

Preheat oven to 180°C (350°F). Line bottom of a 23-cm (9-inch) springform tin with non-stick baking paper.

For Topping: Put walnut pieces in a bowl and sprinkle with brown sugar, flour, and cinnamon. Toss with a fork to combine. Drizzle with melted butter and toss again. Set aside.

For Cake: Cream softened butter and granulated sugar together in a bowl until fluffy. Beat in egg and vanilla. Add sour cream and beat until combined. Sift flour, baking powder, and bicarbonate together. Add to butter mixture and stir until just combined. Pour batter into prepared tin and smooth top. Sprinkle evenly with berries, then with topping.

Bake until cake is risen, golden in colour, no longer jiggles when pan is shaken, and a wooden skewer inserted in centre comes out clean, 55–60 minutes. Remove from oven and let cake stand in tin on a wire rack for 15 minutes before unlatching sides and transferring cake to a plate. Let cool completely, about 2 hours, before slicing.

Note: This cake is best the day it is made but will keep in an airtight container in the refrigerator for several days.

To prepare: 20 minutes

To cook: 55–60 minutes, plus 15 minutes to stand and 2 hours to cool

8–10 servings

baked plums & blackberries

Toss sliced stoned plums and berries with a little vanilla extract and a sprinkling of sugar and bake at 180°C (350°F) until juicy and soft. Serve with a drizzle of cream or a small scoop of berry sorbet, if desired.

purple grape & pistachio ricotta

Mix fresh ricotta with grated lemon zest, vanilla extract, and a little allspice or nutmeg. Sweeten with honey. Serve sprinkled with chopped unsalted pistachios and halved purple grapes or as a spread with crackers and dried figs.

simmered blueberry dessert sauce

For a sauce to accompany ice cream or another dessert, simmer blueberries with 2 Tbsp water and sugar to taste until soft. Mix 1 tsp cornflour with a little orange juice. Add to simmering fruit and stir until slightly thickened.

frozen blackberry yoghurt

Process frozen blackberries or blueberries in a food processor or blender with a squeeze of lemon juice. Add cold yoghurt and process again until blended. If desired, sweeten with a little maple syrup. Freeze until ready to serve.

blackberry granita & cream parfait

Granita

375 g (12 oz) granulated sugar

125 g (4 oz) fresh or frozen blackberries or blackcurrants

60 ml (2 fl oz) lemon juice

Parfait Cream

125 ml (4 fl oz) cold double cream

185 g (6 oz) natural low-fat or whole-milk yoghurt

3 Tbsp icing sugar

2 or 3 small meringues, crumbled (optional)

Fresh blackberries or blackcurrants for garnish (optional)

For Granita: Combine granulated sugar and 750 ml (24 fl oz) water in a non-reactive saucepan and cook over medium heat, stirring until sugar has dissolved. Add berries and bring to a boil. Cook for 5 minutes. Remove from heat and stir in lemon juice. In a blender, purée until smooth. Pour into a large, shallow metal baking dish and freeze until icy, about 4 hours. Break up with a fork and freeze 2 hours more. Break up again, then refreeze. About 2 hours before serving, break up mixture again with a fork and refreeze.

For Parfait Cream: In a bowl, whip cream until soft peaks form when the whisk is lifted. Stir in yoghurt and icing sugar. Cover and chill. To serve, spoon alternating layers of granita and parfait cream into serving glasses, sprinkling crumbled meringue, if using, between layers, and finishing with a layer of parfait cream. If desired, garnish with fresh berries and serve at once.

Notes: All kinds of acid fruits can be added to a sugar syrup base for a granita. Lemon or lime juice works well with a little mint. Store granita in a sealed container in freezer for 4 weeks. Serve without cream if desired.

To cook: 5 minutes

To prepare: 20 minutes, plus at least 8 hours to freeze

6–8 servings

sautéed plums with amaretto

15 g (½ oz) butter

12 large black plums, halved and stoned

125 g (4 oz) sugar

60 ml (2 fl oz) Amaretto liqueur

Greek-style Yoghurt (page 33) for serving

Melt butter in a large frying pan over medium-high heat and cook until starting to brown. Add plums, cut side down, and sprinkle with sugar and Amaretto. Reduce heat to medium-low and cook, shaking pan a couple of times, about 5 minutes. Turn plums and cook 5 minutes more. Turn again and cook until plums start to soften, 3–4 minutes. Do not overcook. Remove to a bowl and let cool. Serve at room temperature, drizzled with liquid from bowl, accompanied by yoghurt.

To prepare: 10 minutes

To cook: 17 minutes

5 or 6 servings

prune compote with greek-style yoghurt

Greek-Style Yoghurt

250 g (8 oz) natural low-fat or whole-milk yoghurt

60 g (2 oz) low-fat sour cream

450 g (1 lb) stoned prunes

500 ml (16 fl oz) hot black tea

250 ml (8 fl oz) red wine or port

250 g (8 oz) sugar

75 g (2½ oz) blanched almonds (optional)

90 g (3 oz) honey

Juice of 1 lemon

2 or 3 orange zest strips

6 cloves

3 cardamom pods, or 1 tsp cardamom seeds

5-cm (2-inch) cinnamon stick

2–3 Tbsp Cognac or brandy (optional)

Freshly grated nutmeg for garnish

For Greek-Style Yoghurt: line a sieve with muslin or a clean, thin kitchen towel and set it over a large bowl. Pour in yoghurt and let drain for 2–3 hours in refrigerator, until thick. Discard liquid. Pour yoghurt into a bowl and mix in sour cream. Refrigerate until ready to use.

Combine all remaining ingredients, except Cognac and nutmeg, in a non-reactive saucepan. Bring to a boil, then reduce heat to maintain a simmer. Cook until fruit is plumped and tender, 15 minutes. Remove from heat and stir in Cognac, if using. Let cool, then chill for at least 2 hours.

If you prefer, remove spices and orange zest strips before serving. Serve prunes in their syrup, garnished with a spoonful of Greek-style yoghurt dusted with nutmeg.

Note: This aromatic compote will keep in refrigerator for up to 2 weeks. It can also be bottled in sterilised jars for longer storage and makes a great Christmas gift. The yoghurt will keep for 3–4 days in refrigerator.

To prepare: 15 minutes, plus 2–3 hours to drain and chill

To cook: 15 minutes

6–8 servings

purple grape tart

1 fully baked 25-cm (10-inch)
Pastry Case (below)

1 egg white, lightly beaten

750 ml (24 fl oz) low-fat or
full-cream milk

4 egg yolks

125 g (4 oz) sugar

2 Tbsp cornflour

1 Tbsp plain flour

1 tsp pure vanilla extract

Grated zest of ½ lemon

2 Tbsp Cognac or brandy (optional)

375 g (12 oz) purple grapes

3 Tbsp grape or cranberry jelly

Preheat oven to 180°C (350°F). Brush inside of baked pastry case with egg white. Bake for 4–5 minutes. Let cool completely.

Heat milk in a saucepan over medium heat to just below a simmer. Whisk egg yolks, sugar, cornflour, flour, vanilla extract, lemon zest, and Cognac, if using, together in a bowl until smooth. Whisk a little hot milk into egg mixture, then gradually stir egg mixture into hot milk. Cook over medium heat, stirring constantly, until smooth and thickened, 2–3 minutes. Remove custard filling from heat and let cool for about 1 hour.

Spread custard evenly in cooled pastry case. Halve and seed grapes and place over custard, cut side down. Chill for at least 20 minutes or up to 6 hours. Just before serving, gently heat jelly, then brush over tart.

Note: Both the pastry case and the custard filling can be prepared ahead of time, but the tart is best glazed just before serving.

To prepare: 20 minutes

*To cook: 15 minutes,
plus 1 hour to cool and
20 minutes–6 hours to chill*

10 servings

pastry case

185 g (6 oz) butter, softened

105 g (3½ oz) caster sugar

2 eggs, lightly beaten

2–3 Tbsp low-fat or full-cream milk

390 g (12½ oz) plain flour

1 tsp baking powder

90 g (3 oz) cornflour

Rapeseed oil cooking spray

Cream butter and sugar until fluffy. Beat in eggs and milk to blend. Stir in dry ingredients until mixture forms a soft ball. Turn out on to a lightly floured work surface and knead lightly. For a 23- or 25-cm (9- or 10-inch) case, divide into thirds. For tartlets, divide each third into 6 pieces. Press each piece into a disc and wrap in clingfilm (see Note).

Roll out a dough disc between 2 sheets of clingfilm to form a round 5 cm (2 inches) larger in diameter than tart tin. Remove plastic from the top and carefully invert dough into a tart or flan tin. Press dough firmly and evenly into tin, ensuring that sides are not too thick. Remove clingfilm and run rolling pin over top to trim. Chill for 10–15 minutes.

Preheat oven to 165°C (325°F). Cover dough with oiled non-stick baking paper or foil. Press evenly into corners of dough and fill with pie weights or dried beans. For a partially baked case, bake for 15 minutes. If paper sticks to pastry, bake for a few more minutes; it should come away easily. Remove paper and weights. For a fully baked case, after removing paper and weights, bake until a pale golden colour, 15–20 minutes more.

Note: This recipe makes dough for multiple tarts, which you can refrigerate for up to 1 week or freeze for up to 6 months.

*To prepare: 30 minutes, plus
10 minutes to chill*

To cook: about 30 minutes

*Three 23-cm (9-inch) or
25-cm (10-inch) pastry cases
or eighteen 11.5-cm (4½-inch)
pastry cases*

honeydew melons green pears

GREEN FRUITS AND VEGETABLES BOOST THE IMMUNE

fresh mint avocados key limes

SYSTEM • PROMOTE EYE HEALTH • HELP BUILD STRONG

green apples kiwi fruits persian

BONES • BUILD STRONG TEETH • OFFER ANTIOXIDANTS

limes green grapes fresh basil

FOR HEALING AND PROTECTION • REDUCE THE RISK OF

honeydew melons green pears

CERTAIN CANCERS • GREEN FRUITS AND VEGETABLES

fresh mint avocados key limes

BOOST THE IMMUNE SYSTEM • PROMOTE EYE HEALTH

Green

Green is the colour of growing things. The flavour of green fruits is light, fresh, and clean and their texture is crisp and juicy. They are naturally good for you, and since so many fruits are green, you'll find a good variety available year-round, not just a brief summertime explosion. Green tea and green herbs both share the antioxidant benefits of green fruits, and make interesting additions to a dessert.

In the heat of midsummer, green fruits such as honeydew melon and green grapes make cool and refreshing finishes to a light supper. Frozen grapes (see Green Tea Punch, page 41) make a simple, fun dessert or snack on their own. Or turn to page 47 for a very easy salad that pairs juicy green melon with luscious avocado.

The appearance of apples and pears at farmers' markets is a sure sign that autumn is arriving, the weather is turning cool and it's time to start baking. A spiced apple cake is a classic winter dessert (page 41). Pears are so elegant that even simply baking them with a spice-and-nut filling makes an impressive finale to a meal (page 45).

The winter months bring tropical kiwi fruits and bright, cheery citrus fruits such as lemons and limes. You can combine the complementary flavours of both in a pretty tart or tartlet (page 48). Kiwi fruit Sorbet (page 42), sharpened with lemon juice, offers a light and fresh alternative to the usual rich ice cream flavours.

SPRING	SUMMER	AUTUMN	WINTER
green apples	green apples	green apples	green apples
avocados	avocados	green grapes	avocados
green grapes	green grapes	herbs	green grapes
herbs	herbs	kiwi fruits	kiwi fruits
kiwi fruits	green pears	Persian limes	Persian limes
Persian and Key limes	Persian and Key limes	green-fleshed melons	green pears
green-fleshed melons	green melons	green pears	green tea
green pears	green tea	green tea	
green tea			

spiced apple cake

3 green apples

250 g (8 oz) granulated sugar

125 g (4 oz) butter, melted

1 egg

200 g (6½ oz) plain flour

1 tsp bicarbonate of soda

1 tsp ground cinnamon

½ tsp freshly grated nutmeg

½ tsp ground allspice

½ tsp salt

90 g (3 oz) sultanas

2 Tbsp granulated sugar mixed with 1 tsp ground cinnamon

Icing sugar for dusting

Preheat oven to 165°C (325°F). Butter a 20-cm (8-inch) diameter round cake tin. Core and thinly slice apples, leaving skin intact. Beat granulated sugar, butter, and egg together in a bowl. Stir in two-thirds of the apple slices.

Sift flour, bicarbonate of soda, cinnamon, nutmeg, allspice, and salt together. Add to egg mixture with the sultanas, stirring until just blended. Pour into prepared tin and smooth top. Arrange remaining apple slices in a pattern on top, pressing them gently into batter. Sprinkle with cinnamon sugar. Bake until golden and springy to touch, about 50 minutes. Let cake stand in tin on a wire rack for 10 minutes, then turn out and let cool completely, about 2 hours. Dust with icing sugar and cut into wedges to serve.

Notes: You can use any type of apples in season. The cake will taste slightly different every time but it is always moist, as well as easy to prepare. Store cake in a covered container in refrigerator for up to 4 days.

To prepare: 20 minutes

To cook: 50 minutes, plus 10 minutes to stand and 2 hours to cool

8–10 servings

green tea punch

560 g (3 cups/18 oz) seedless green grapes

4 tsp best-quality green tea leaves, or 6 green tea bags

2 Tbsp sugar

250 ml (1 cup/8 fl oz) pineapple juice

250 ml (1 cup/8 fl oz) ginger beer or ginger ale

2 Tbsp lime juice

Put grapes on a baking sheet and freeze for at least 2 hours. (To freeze longer, transfer to a covered container.) Bring 1.5 l (2 pints 8 fl oz) water to a boil, let stand for 1 minute, then pour it over tea leaves and sugar in a teapot. Let stand for 2–3 minutes. Strain into a bowl, let cool, and chill.

To serve, stir pineapple juice, ginger beer, and lime juice into cold tea. Pour into a jug or into individual glasses and add frozen grapes.

To prepare: 10 minutes, plus 2 hours to chill and freeze

6–8 servings

kiwi fruit sorbet

6 kiwi fruits, peeled

155 g (5 oz) sugar

125 ml (4 fl oz) lemon juice

12 fresh mint leaves, thinly sliced

1 egg white

3 Tbsp Cointreau or other liqueur of choice (optional)

Garnish
Lemon zest strips
Sliced peeled kiwi fruits

Purée kiwi fruits in a blender just until smooth. Do not overblend, or seeds will break up and make purée bitter. Measure out 500 ml (16 fl oz) purée. Set aside.

Combine sugar and 375 ml (12 fl oz) water in a saucepan and bring to a boil over medium heat, stirring to dissolve sugar. Simmer syrup for 5 minutes. Let cool and chill for 2 hours.

In a bowl, mix kiwi purée with lemon juice, mint, and cold syrup. Pour into a shallow metal baking tin and freeze until icy, about 4 hours. Process in a food processor or beat with an electric mixer until smooth. Add egg white and liqueur, if using, and process or beat until fluffy. Refreeze until firm, about 4 hours, then beat again. Pack sorbet into a container and freeze completely, 4 hours more. Serve in chilled glasses, garnished with lemon zest and sliced kiwi fruits.

To prepare: 30 minutes, plus 2 hours to chill and 12 hours to freeze

To cook: 5 minutes

6–8 servings

silky lime mousse

155 g (5 oz) low-fat or whole-milk natural yoghurt

3 eggs, separated

Finely grated zest of 3 limes

4–6 Tbsp lime juice (about 4 limes)

75 g (2½ oz) caster sugar

1½ tsp unflavoured powdered gelatine

160 ml (5 fl oz) cold double cream

Line a sieve with muslin or use a clean thin kitchen towel and set it over a large bowl. Pour in yoghurt and let drain for 2–3 hours in refrigerator, until thick. Discard liquid.

Combine yolks, lime zest and juice, and half the sugar in a large heatproof bowl and set over a saucepan containing 5 cm (2 inches) of simmering water. Whisk constantly until yolks are pale and thickened. Remove bowl from pan and set aside.

Sprinkle gelatine over 60 ml (2 fl oz) cold water and let stand until absorbed, about 3 minutes. Heat in microwave oven for 30–40 seconds or in a saucepan on the hob for 1–2 minutes to dissolve. Stir to ensure that gelatine is fully dissolved. Whisk into lime mixture. Chill until mixture starts to set, about 40 minutes.

In a bowl, whip cream until soft peaks form when the whisk is lifted and fold into lime mixture. Fold in yoghurt. In a large bowl, beat egg whites until foaming, then gradually beat in remaining sugar until soft peaks form. Fold lime mixture into beaten whites. Spoon into individual dishes or a large serving dish. Chill until set, about 3 hours, then serve.

To prepare: 20 minutes, plus 3 hours to drain yoghurt and 3¾ hours to set mousse

To cook: 5 minutes

6 servings

baked apples with caramel sauce

6 large green-skinned apples such as Granny Smith

60 g (2 oz) dried cranberries or dried cherries

30 g (1 oz) pecans or walnuts, chopped

½ tsp ground cinnamon

½ tsp ground allspice

¼ tsp freshly grated nutmeg

Caramel Sauce

250 g (8 oz) sugar

170 ml (5½ fl oz) light corn syrup or golden syrup

1 Tbsp lemon juice

2 Tbsp butter

Preheat oven to 180°C (350°F). Using an apple corer, cut out cores from apples in neat plugs. Use a paring knife to enlarge each cavity to 2.5 cm (1 inch) in diameter. Cut a thin ring of peel around circumference of each apple with knife. Place apples in a shallow baking dish. Stir cranberries, nuts, and spices together in a bowl. Divide mixture evenly among apples, stuffing into cavities.

For Caramel Sauce: Combine sugar, 3 Tbsp water, corn syrup or golden syrup, and lemon juice in a non-reactive saucepan and bring to a boil over medium heat. Cook until sauce turns a rich amber colour, about 15 minutes, brushing inside of pan with a wet pastry brush to prevent mixture from crystallising. Remove from heat and stir in butter until smooth.

Pour hot sauce over apples. Bake until apples are wrinkly and soft, 30–35 minutes. Serve hot, topped with caramel sauce.

To prepare: 30 minutes

To cook: 45–60 minutes

6 servings

stuffed green pears

4 green-skinned pears, stems intact

75 g (2½ oz) almonds, chopped

75 g (2½ oz) ground almonds

2 Tbsp packed soft brown sugar

Grated zest of ½ lemon

1 tsp ground cloves

1 egg white

170 ml (5½ fl oz) maple syrup

Preheat oven to 165°C (325°F). Using an apple corer or teaspoon, cut out cores from bottom of pears (leaving a little of the core at the top will help keep stem attached). Use a teaspoon to enlarge each cavity enough to hold 2 Tbsp filling.

Stir chopped almonds, ground almonds, sugar, lemon zest, cloves, and egg white together in a small bowl. Divide mixture evenly among pears, pressing firmly into cavities. Stand pears in a shallow baking dish (if necessary, cut slices from the bottoms so they stand upright). Drizzle with maple syrup. Cover tightly with foil and bake until pears are easily pierced with a skewer, about 1 hour. To serve, place pears on plates and spoon syrup on top.

To prepare: 15 minutes

To cook: 1 hour

4 servings

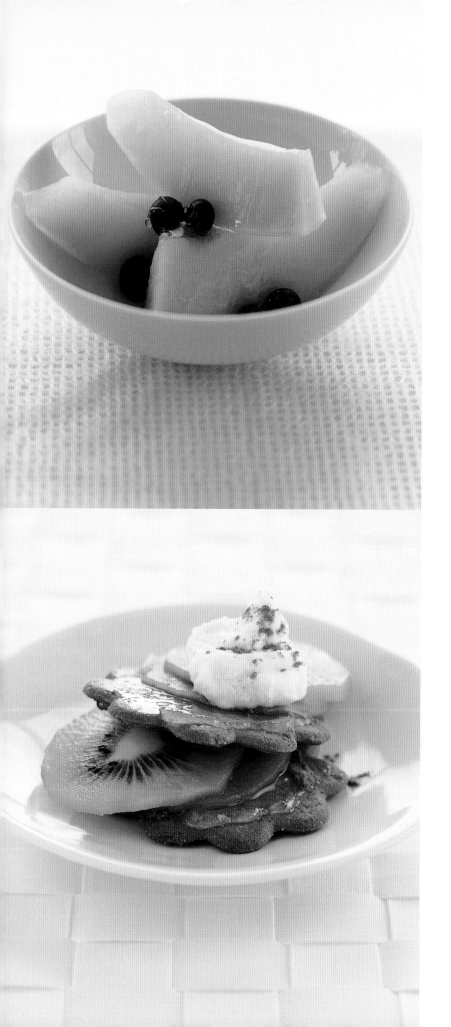

melon in spiced syrup

Combine equal amounts of sugar and water in a pan and stir over medium heat until sugar dissolves. Add grated ginger, star anise, and lemon zest and juice and simmer gently for 10 minutes. Cool, strain, and serve over sliced honeydew.

kiwi fruit sandwiches

Spread thin, crisp biscuits, such as ginger snaps, with apricot jam. Layer with sliced kiwi fruit and top with ricotta cheese flavoured with a little lemon juice, honey, and cinnamon.

baked fruit parcels

Place grape, pear, and kiwi slices on non-stick baking paper. Drizzle with honey, scatter with finely chopped ginger, add whole spices such as cardamom, star anise, or cinnamon, and wrap. Bake at 180°C (350°F) for about 30 minutes.

avocado & melon salad

Combine chunks of just-ripe avocado and green-fleshed melon and spoon into serving glasses over thick Greek-Style Yoghurt (page 33). Drizzle with honey and plenty of lime or lemon juice.

kiwi fruit tart with lime curd filling

Lime Curd

250 g (8 oz) sugar

185 g (6 oz) plus 2 Tbsp butter, diced

Grated zest of 3 limes

125 ml (4 fl oz) lime juice

4 eggs, lightly beaten

1 fully baked 25-cm (10-inch) Pastry Case or 6 individual Pastry Cases (page 34)

1 egg white, lightly beaten

4 or 5 kiwi fruits, peeled and thinly sliced

3 Tbsp apricot jam or passion fruit syrup

For Lime Curd: Combine sugar, butter, and lime zest and juice in a non-reactive saucepan and bring to a boil over medium heat, stirring to dissolve sugar. Remove from heat, whisk in eggs, and pour into a heatproof bowl. Set over a saucepan containing 5 cm (2 inches) simmering water. Stir constantly until mixture is thick enough to coat the back of a spoon, 6–8 minutes. (If you have a sugar thermometer, you can cook mixture directly over low heat. Stir constantly just until it reaches 77°C/170°F. Remove from heat and stir for a minute.) Let cool, cover surface with non-stick baking paper to prevent a skin from forming, and chill until ready to use.

Preheat oven to 180°C (350°F). Brush inside of baked pastry case with egg white. Bake for 4–5 minutes to set egg white. Let cool completely on a wire rack.

Spoon chilled lime curd into cooled pastry case and arrange sliced kiwi fruits on top. Gently heat jam and strain to remove any solids. Brush over tart to glaze. Serve at once.

Notes: The tart(s) can be assembled without glaze up to 8 hours ahead. Brush with glaze just before serving. The curd keeps well in a covered container in refrigerator for up to 10 days. It can also be bottled in sterilised jars for longer storage and gift giving.

To prepare: 15 minutes

To cook: 5 minutes

8 servings

minted green tea jellies with kiwi fruit

4 tsp unflavoured powdered gelatine

60 g (2 oz) sugar

1 tsp green tea powder

12 fresh mint leaves

2 kiwi fruits, peeled and finely diced

Juice of 1 lime

In a cup, sprinkle gelatine over 2 Tbsp cold water and let stand until absorbed, about 3 minutes. Heat in a microwave oven for 20 seconds or in a small saucepan over low heat on the hob for about 1 minute to dissolve. Stir to ensure that gelatine is fully dissolved.

In a bowl, combine sugar and green tea powder. Stir in 2 Tbsp water to form a paste.

In a saucepan, bring 500 ml (16 fl oz) water to a boil and pour over mint in a heatproof bowl. Let stand for 2 minutes, then strain and add mint-flavoured water to tea paste along with gelatine mixture. Discard mint. Stir until sugar is completely dissolved.

Divide mixture among four 125-ml (4–fl oz) serving glasses or bowls. Chill until set, about 5 hours, stirring several times before mixture sets to prevent separating. Just before serving, garnish with diced kiwi fruits and drizzle with a little fresh lime juice.

Notes: These jellies are set very loosely. If you prefer a firmer set, increase quantity of gelatine. Kiwi fruits contain an enzyme that prevents setting, so don't garnish jellies until ready to serve, or they will break down.

To prepare: 20 minutes, plus at least 5 hours to chill

4 servings

ginger white peaches tan pears

WHITE AND TAN FRUITS AND VEGETABLES CONTAIN

bananas dates white nectarines

ANTIOXIDANTS FOR HEALING AND PROTECTION • HELP

dried white peaches white corn

MAINTAIN A HEALTHY CHOLESTEROL LEVEL • PROMOTE

ginger tan figs white peaches

HEART HEALTH • BOOST THE IMMUNE SYSTEM • SLOW

tan pears bananas dates white

CHOLESTEROL ABSORPTION • WHITE AND TAN FRUITS

nectarines dried white peaches

AND VEGETABLES OFFER ANTIOXIDANTS FOR HEALING

White & tan

Eating a healthy diet means eating a wide variety of foods, constantly changing your body's sources of energy and nutrients to get the broadest range possible. White foods like refined sugar and flour may be less than desirable, but white and tan fruits offer an array of coveted benefits. If you include the dried forms, some fruits in this colour group are available year-round.

Bananas are white – at least the part you eat – and are a most versatile fruit. They make a good addition to breakfast cereal and a convenient self-contained snack at any time of day. But don't overlook them as a dessert ingredient. They give baked goods such as Streusel Banana Muffins (page 68) an appealing moistness and provide nutritious substance for an updated banana split with Asian flavours (page 62).

Considered a tan food, fresh ginger is valued as a traditional medicine for its stomach-settling properties. These effects make ginger a good counter-balance to a rich dinner, so it has long been a favourite ingredient in desserts. Here, the warm, spicy flavour of gingerbread is intensified by using two forms of ginger in one recipe (page 61): ground and crystallised.

In summer, you'll want to make the most of juicy fresh peaches and nectarines while they last, in rustic tarts (page 67), or by brushing the fruits with honey and roasting them (page 63).

SPRING	SUMMER	AUTUMN	WINTER
bananas	bananas	bananas	dates
dried tan figs	tan figs	dates	dried tan figs
ginger	white nectarines	tan figs	ginger
dried white nectarines	white peaches	ginger	dried white nectarines
dried white peaches	white sweetcorn	dried white nectarines	dried white peaches
tan-skinned pears		dried white peaches	tan pears
		tan pears	

ginger angel
food cakes

60 g (2 oz) soft-wheat flour

½ tsp baking powder

150 g (5 oz) caster sugar

6 large egg whites

¾ tsp cream of tartar

Pinch of salt

1 Tbsp finely grated fresh ginger

1 tsp pure vanilla extract

Grated zest of ½ lemon

Ginger Icing

125 g (4 oz) icing sugar

1 Tbsp lemon juice

1 Tbsp finely chopped ginger in syrup
or crystallised ginger

1 Tbsp syrup from ginger in syrup
or ginger tea

Preheat oven to 180°C (350°F). Sift flour, baking powder, and 90 g (3 oz) caster sugar together 3 times.

In a large bowl, beat egg whites with cream of tartar and salt until soft peaks form when the whisk is lifted. Add ginger, vanilla, and lemon zest. Gradually beat in remaining 60 g (2 oz) sugar until dissolved. Using a large slotted spoon, gently fold in dry ingredients just until evenly blended.

Spoon batter into 6 non-stick cups of a large bun tin, or 10 standard patty-pan or deep cupcake pans. Bake until cakes are springy to the touch, 25–30 minutes.

For Icing: In a bowl, combine icing sugar and lemon juice. Stir in finely chopped ginger and ginger syrup or ginger tea to make a runny icing.

Remove cakes from oven, invert on to a wire rack, and let cool completely. Remove from pan. Spoon a little icing over each cake, and serve.

Note: Store cakes in an airtight container for up to 3 days.

To prepare: 20 minutes

To cook: 25–30 minutes

6 or 10 individual cakes

caramelised bananas

45 g (1½ oz) butter

60 g (2 oz) brown sugar

250 ml (8 fl oz) apple or
pineapple juice

2 Tbsp lime juice

6–8 small finger bananas or
3 or 4 regular bananas, peeled and
halved lengthways

Vanilla frozen yoghurt for serving

Melt butter in a frying pan over medium heat and cook until it bubbles and starts to brown. Add sugar, apple juice, and lime juice. Cook over medium-high heat until syrupy, 8–10 minutes. Reduce heat to medium, add bananas, and cook until slightly softened, 3–4 minutes, turning gently with tongs to cook both sides. Serve bananas in their sauce, accompanied by vanilla frozen yoghurt.

To prepare: 15 minutes

To cook: 15 minutes

3 or 4 servings

sauternes-poached pears

4–6 firm tan-skinned pears, stems intact

750 ml (24 fl oz) Sauternes or other
dessert wine

125 g (4 oz) sugar

1 cinnamon stick

2 bay leaves

Choose a pot that will hold pears fairly snugly when fruits stand upright. Set pears aside and heat Sauternes and sugar in pot over medium heat, stirring until sugar is dissolved. Add pears, cinnamon, and bay leaves, arranging pears so they are submerged as far as possible in syrup. Cover pears with a circle of non-stick baking paper slightly larger than pot to help keep them moist.

Return liquid to a simmer, then reduce heat to low, cover, and cook pears very gently until tender, about 40 minutes, turning several times so they cook evenly. Carefully lift pears from syrup with a slotted spoon. Raise heat to high and boil syrup to reduce it a little and concentrate flavours, about 5 minutes. Serve pears warm or cold with a little syrup.

Notes: Pears can be cooked, covered, and refrigerated for up to 4 days in syrup (this actually improves their flavour). If you prefer pears served warm, reheat gently in the syrup. Leftover syrup can be used to cook more pears or stone fruits.

To prepare: 5 minutes

To cook: 45 minutes

4–6 servings

crystallised-ginger gingerbread

60 g (2 oz) butter, softened

125 g (4 oz) granulated sugar

170 ml (5½ fl oz) molasses

90 g (3 oz) crystallised ginger

2 eggs at room temperature

235 g (7½ oz) plain flour

1 tsp bicarbonate of soda

2 tsp ground ginger

½ tsp ground cinnamon

½ tsp ground allspice

¼ tsp freshly grated nutmeg

125 ml (4 fl oz) buttermilk or low-fat or whole-milk yoghurt

Demerara or coffee sugar crystals for sprinkling (optional)

Preheat oven to 180°C (350°F). Butter a 23 x 10-cm (9 x 4-inch) loaf pan and line bottom with non-stick baking paper.

Cream butter and granulated sugar together in a bowl until fluffy. Stir in molasses and finely chopped ginger. Beat in eggs one at a time. Sift dry ingredients together. Stir into butter mixture in 3 additions alternately with buttermilk in 2 additions, mixing until smooth.

Pour into prepared pan and smooth top. Bake until gingerbread is golden and springy to the touch and a skewer inserted in centre comes out clean, 45–50 minutes. Let gingerbread stand in pan on a wire rack for 10 minutes. Turn out and serve warm or at room temperature, sprinkled with demerara or coffee crystal sugar, if using.

Notes: This tender, moist, dark gingerbread is good served warm with poached pears and their syrup (page 58) or a bowl of Greek-style yoghurt (page 33). Or, try it with afternoon tea or coffee. Store in an airtight container for up to 1 week.

To prepare: 10 minutes

To cook: 45–50 minutes

1 large loaf, 10–12 servings

white nectarines with lychees & grapes

4 perfectly ripe white nectarines

2 cups (12 oz/375 g) seedless green grapes

1 can (18 oz/560 g) lychees in juice

1 Tbsp lime juice

Halve, pit, and thinly slice nectarines. Halve grapes. Drain lychees, reserving juice, and finely dice.

Pour reserved lychee juice into a serving bowl. Add prepared fruit to bowl, sprinkle with lime juice, and mix gently to combine.

Chill for at least 1 hour or up to 4 hours before serving.

To prepare: 15 minutes, plus 1 hour to chill

6 servings

labneh with ginger, grapes & almonds

Drain yoghurt overnight in a lined sieve (see page 33) to produce soft labneh cheese. Mix with icing sugar and lemon juice to taste. Serve with chopped crystallised ginger, grapes, toasted almonds, and sliced tan pears.

banana-coconut split

Update a classic banana split with sliced bananas, peeled or canned lychees, a scoop of coconut ice cream, and a drizzle of purchased or homemade passion fruit or mango sauce. Garnish with toasted dessicated or fresh grated

roasted white nectarines

Halve and stone white nectarines and brush with honey or sprinkle with brown sugar. Toast in a hot oven or under grill until browned and caramelised. Serve with a garnish of cream or crème fraîche and thyme or lavender, if desired.

kaffir-infused pears

Kaffir lime leaves have a tropical flavour that complements fruit well. Toss finely shredded Kaffir lime leaves and mint leaves with sliced tan-skinned pears such as Bosc and/or Asian pears. Stir in a little lime juice and sugar to taste.

fresh dates with pistachio-mascarpone filling

Pistachio-Mascarpone Filling

90 g (3 oz) raisins

90 g (3 oz) dried figs

30 g (1 oz) pistachio nuts

45 g (1½ oz) dried apricots

2 Tbsp finely chopped crystallised ginger

125 g (4 oz) mascarpone cheese

Grated zest of ½ lemon

½ tsp ground cardamom

25 fresh dates or figs

For Filling: Finely chop raisins, dried figs, pistachios and apricots. Combine in a bowl with ginger, mascarpone, lemon zest, and cardamom and stir to blend.

Split dates along one side and remove stones, or cut a notch in top of each fresh fig. Fill each date or fig with 1 tsp filling. Serve at once, or refrigerate until ready to serve.

Note: Filled dates and figs will keep in a covered container in refrigerator for up to 3 days.

To prepare: 20 minutes

4 servings

brandied baked figs

12–14 large tan-skinned figs

½ lemon, very thinly sliced (unpeeled)

12-mm (½-inch) piece fresh ginger, peeled and very thinly sliced

3 oz (90 g) sugar

125 ml (4 fl oz) brandy

Crème fraîche or mascarpone for serving (optional)

Preheat oven to 150°C (300°F). Arrange the figs in a baking dish that holds them fairly snugly. Scatter lemon and ginger slices on top. Sprinkle with sugar and drizzle with brandy. Wrap dish tightly in foil and bake until figs are very tender, about 1½ hours, turning once after 1 hour. Let cool on a wire rack, then chill for at least 2 hours before serving. Accompany figs with their brandied cooking syrup and crème fraîche, if using.

Note: Store figs in their syrup in refrigerator for up to 1 week.

To prepare: 10 minutes

To cook: 1½ hours, plus 2 hours to chill

4–6 servings

white peach crostatas

½ recipe Cornmeal Pastry (page 79)

2 large or 3 medium white peaches, halved, stoned, and very thinly sliced (about 20 slices per peach)

2 Tbsp lemon juice

60 g (2 oz) granulated sugar

1 Tbsp icing sugar for dusting

Preheat oven to 200°C (400°F). Roll out pastry on a lightly floured work surface to 3 mm (⅛ inch) thick. Cut into six 15-cm (6-inch) rounds, re-rolling pastry as needed. Place rounds on a baking sheet, allowing a little space between them. Fan peach slices in a ring in centre of each round, leaving a 12-mm (½-inch) margin around edge. Fold in edge to slightly enclose peaches, crimping gently with your fingers to hold pastry together where it overlaps. Brush peaches with lemon juice and sprinkle with granulated sugar. Bake until golden, about 35 minutes. Serve warm or at room temperature, dusted with icing sugar.

Note: Don't worry if peaches turn brown as they are being prepared; they will brown further during cooking as the sugar caramelises. These crostatas are best eaten the day they are made.

To prepare: 20 minutes, plus 40 minutes for pastry

To cook: 35 minutes

6 servings

sweetcorn bread

315 g (10 oz) plain flour

220 g (7 oz) instant polenta

125 g (4 oz) sugar

2 tsp baking powder

1 tsp bicarbonate of soda

½ tsp salt

250 ml (8 fl oz) buttermilk

2 Tbsp maple syrup

2 eggs

125 ml (4 fl oz) rapeseed oil

2 ripe bananas, mashed

90 g (3 oz) white sweetcorn kernels

Butter a 23 x 13–cm (9 x 5–inch) loaf tin and line bottom with non-stick baking paper. Preheat oven to 180°C (350°F). Stir flour, polenta, sugar, baking powder, bicarbonate of soda, and salt together in a bowl until blended. Whisk buttermilk, maple syrup, eggs, and oil together in another bowl. Stir in bananas, then add to dry ingredients with corn kernels and stir until just combined (do not overmix). Pour into prepared pan and smooth top. Bake until loaf is risen and firm to the touch and a skewer inserted in centre comes out clean, about 50 minutes. Let sweetcorn bread stand in pan on a wire rack for 15 minutes, then turn out on to rack to cool completely, about 1 hour. Slice and serve.

Note: Use fresh or canned yellow sweetcorn kernels if you cannot find white ones. If you cannot get buttermilk, use live yoghurt.

To prepare: 15 minutes

To cook: 50 minutes, plus 15 minutes to stand and 1 hour to cool

6–8 servings

streusel banana muffins

Streusel Topping

60 g (2 oz) plain flour

60 g (2 oz) packed brown sugar

60 g (2 oz) butter, melted

30 g (1 oz) chopped almonds

Muffin Mixture

315 g (10 oz) plain flour

115 g (3¾ oz) bran flakes or wheat bran

3 tsp baking powder

3 tsp ground cinnamon

1 tsp ground ginger

250 ml (8 fl oz) low-fat or full-cream milk

45 g (1½ oz) butter

3 Tbsp light corn or golden syrup

105 g (3½ oz) soft brown sugar

1 tsp bicarbonate of soda

2 ripe large bananas, mashed

Preheat oven to 200°C (400°F). Butter a 12-cup muffin tin.

For Streusel Topping: In a bowl, combine flour and sugar and toss with a fork to blend. Drizzle 4 Tbsp melted butter over and stir in almonds. Set aside.

Stir flour, bran, baking powder, cinnamon, and ginger together in a large bowl and stir with a fork to blend.

Combine milk, butter, corn syrup or golden syrup, and sugar in a microwave-proof bowl and heat in microwave or in a saucepan over medium heat on hob until butter is melted and sugar is dissolved, about 2 minutes in microwave or 4–5 minutes on hob. Stir in bicarbonate of soda and mashed bananas. Add wet ingredients to dry ingredients and mix until just combined. Do not overmix.

Spoon batter into prepared muffin tin. Sprinkle with streusel topping. Bake until muffins are risen and golden, 15–20 minutes. Let muffins stand in pan on a wire rack for 2–3 minutes, then turn out and serve.

Notes: If you have overripe bananas, this is a good way to use them. Make a batch of muffin mixture, store it in the refrigerator, and bake a few muffins at a time so that you can enjoy fresh muffins throughout the week with very little effort. The baked muffins also freeze well. Corn syrup is available from shops that sell American foods.

To prepare: 15 minutes

To cook: 15–20 minutes

12 muffins

apricots yellow apples mangoes

YELLOW AND ORANGE FRUITS AND VEGETABLES HELP

grapefruit peaches pineapples

PROMOTE HEART HEALTH • HELP REDUCE THE RISK OF

yellow gooseberries nectarines

CERTAIN CANCERS • PROMOTE EYE HEALTH • CONTAIN

pumpkins oranges persimmons

ANTIOXIDANTS FOR HEALING AND PROTECTION • BOOST

carrots sweet potatoes lemons

THE IMMUNE SYSTEM • YELLOW AND ORANGE FRUITS

golden kiwi fruits dried apricots

AND VEGETABLES OFFER ANTIOXIDANTS FOR HEALING

Yellow & orange

Nutritionists have long known that yellow and orange fruits and vegetables are excellent sources of the antioxidant beta-carotene, which the body converts into essential vitamin A, but only recently have the full benefits of this colour group come to light. Orange fruits and vegetables taste bright and zesty, and they help keep us healthy in many ways throughout the year.

Orange and yellow citrus fruits make several appearances in this chapter, and not only in the most common forms. For a change of pace, try tiny kumquats preserved in brandy (page 81) or a simple ice cream made from the mild Meyer lemon, a hybrid of lemon and mandarin orange (page 75). Many citrus fruits come into season in autumn and winter, offering the cold-fighting benefits of vitamin C just when we most need them.

The stone fruits of summer – peaches, nectarines, and apricots – are a fleeting pleasure. Enjoy them during their brief season as part of a simple tart (page 79) or an even simpler dessert of poached fruit with a tart raspberry sauce (page 80).

Orange vegetables are among the handful that play regular roles in baked desserts. Carrots make moist and sweet cupcakes (page 82). Sweet potatoes contribute generous doses of vitamins A, C, and E to the diet, as well as antioxidants. Enjoy these benefits in a sweet potato pie (page 86) with a crunchy digestive biscuit crust.

SPRING	SUMMER	AUTUMN	WINTER
yellow apples	apricots	yellow apples	yellow apples
apricots	dried apricots	dried apricots	dried apricots
dried apricots	carrots	carrots	carrots
carrots	yellow gooseberries	golden kiwi fruits	grapefruits
grapefruits	lemons	lemons	golden kiwi fruits
golden kiwi fruit	mangoes	yellow- & orange-fleshed melons	kumquats
kumquat	yellow- & orange-fleshed melons	navel & mandarin oranges	lemons
lemons	nectarines	papayas	navel & mandarin oranges
mangoes	Valencia oranges	yellow pears	yellow pears
navel & mandarin oranges	peaches	persimmons	pumpkins
papayas	golden raspberries	pumpkins	sweet potatoes
pineapples	sweetcorn	sweet potatoes	
sweetcorn			

meyer lemon meringue ice cream

330 g (10½ oz) caster sugar

Grated zest of 1 Meyer lemon or other
sweet lemon (see Notes)

125–160 ml (4–5 fl oz) Meyer lemon juice,
strained (see Notes)

4 egg whites

250 ml (8 fl oz) double cream

Combine sugar, lemon zest, and lemon juice in a small saucepan. Cook over low heat, stirring, until sugar is dissolved. Raise heat to medium-high and cook until mixture reaches consistency of a thick syrup and large bubbles form as it boils, about 5 minutes. Mixture is ready when it reaches 110°C (225°F) on a sugar thermometer.

With an electric mixer on medium speed, beat egg whites until stiff, glossy peaks form when whisk is lifted. On low speed, gradually add hot syrup and beat until cool and very thick, about 10 minutes.

In a deep bowl, beat cream until soft peaks form. Using a large, flat spoon, fold into egg white mixture until evenly blended. Place in a freezer-proof container, cover, and freeze until firm, about 4 hours.

Notes: An ice-cream maker is not needed to produce this creamy, smooth ice cream. If you cannot find Meyer lemons or other sweet lemons such as limettas, which are occasionally available in specialist shops, use ordinary lemons but reduce juice quantity to 125 ml (4 fl oz) and increase sugar to 390 g (12½ oz). Two or three Tbsp limoncello or other lemon liqueur may be added to the whipped cream; it will make the ice cream slightly softer. Store in freezer for up to 4 weeks.

To prepare: 40 minutes

*To cook: 5 minutes, plus
at least 4 hours to freeze*

1.5 liters/2¾ pints, 6 servings

orange & sabayon gratin

2 egg yolks

90 g (3 oz) sugar

180 ml (6 fl oz) Muscat, or sweet
white sparkling wine

2 Tbsp double cream

5 oranges, peeled and segmented

Whisk egg yolks and sugar together in a heatproof bowl until very pale and thick. Whisk in wine. Set bowl over a saucepan containing 5 cm (2 inches) simmering water. Whisk constantly until mixture is thick enough to coat the back of a spoon, about 5 minutes. Transfer bowl to a larger bowl of ice water to stop the cooking process. Whisk in cream. Use at once, or cover and chill.

To serve, preheat a grill. Divide orange segments among 4 individual gratin dishes. Whisk sabayon and pour over fruit. Place under the grill and cook just until sabayon starts to turn golden, 2–3 minutes.

Note: Sabayon will keep, refrigerated, for up to 24 hours.

To prepare: 25 minutes

To cook: 2–3 minutes

4 servings

papaya & mango tapioca

90 g (3 oz) small pearl tapioca

60 ml (2 fl oz) unsweetened coconut cream

2 Tbsp granulated sugar

1 large mango, peeled and diced

½ medium or large papaya, peeled, seeded, and sliced

Juice of 1 lime

4 tsp muscovado sugar, or grated palm sugar (jaggery)

Bring 1 l (1¾ pints) water to a boil over high heat. Reduce heat to a simmer, add tapioca, and cook until translucent, 12–15 minutes. Drain thoroughly through a fine-meshed sieve. Put in a bowl and stir in coconut cream and granulated sugar, stirring to dissolve sugar. Cover and chill for at least 1 hour or up to 24 hours.

Divide among individual serving bowls and top with fruit. Drizzle with lime juice and sprinkle with muscovado or palm sugar.

Note: Pearl tapioca can be found in healthfood stores. This is quite a rich dessert, so the servings are small.

To prepare: 20 minutes

To cook: 15 minutes, plus 1 hour to chill

4 servings

honey-glazed pineapple

1 large pineapple

125 g (4 oz) honey

6 star anise

Lime wedges for garnish

Cut peel from pineapple, trim away eyes, and halve lengthways. Remove core from pineapple halves and cut each half crossways into 8–10 slices 2.5 cm (1 inch) thick. Put in a shallow baking dish, drizzle with honey, and scatter with star anise. Let stand at room temperature to macerate for at least 30 minutes or refrigerate for up to 4 hours. Turn pineapple slices halfway through macerating time.

Preheat the grill. Line a baking sheet with foil, arrange pineapple in a single layer, and grill until lightly browned, about 5 minutes per side. Serve hot, topped with cooking juices and star anise, and garnished with lime wedges for squeezing.

To prepare: 20 minutes

To cook: 10 minutes, plus 30 minutes to macerate

4 servings

roasted apricot & vanilla tart

½ recipe Cornmeal Pastry (below)

1 egg white, lightly beaten

90 g (3 oz) apricot jam

1 tsp cornflour

8–10 firm, ripe apricots, stoned and cut into eighths

1 tsp pure vanilla extract

1 Tbsp caster sugar

1 Tbsp icing sugar

Preheat oven to 180°C (350°F). Roll out dough between 2 sheets of clingfilm to form a round 30 cm (12 inches) in diameter. Remove top sheet of clingfilm and carefully invert dough into a 25-cm (10-inch) tart tin. Press dough firmly and evenly into pan, ensuring that sides are not too thick. Run rolling pin over top to trim. Chill for 30 minutes in refrigerator or 10 minutes in freezer. Cover dough with a round of non-stick baking paper or foil and fill with pie weights or dried beans. Bake until pastry is set, 20 minutes. Remove paper and weights and bake until lightly coloured, 10 minutes more (line edges with foil if they are browning too fast). Brush with egg white and bake for 5 minutes more. Let cool on a wire rack.

Stir apricot jam and cornflour together in a small bowl. Spread in pastry shell and arrange apricots on top. Stir vanilla and superfine sugar together and sprinkle over apricots. Bake until fruit is tender and bubbling, about 35 minutes. Serve warm or chilled, dusted with icing sugar.

To prepare: 20 minutes, plus 40 minutes for pastry

To cook: 70 minutes

8 servings

cornmeal pastry

185 g (6 oz) cold butter, finely diced

470 g (15 oz) plain flour

105 g (3½ oz) coarse cornmeal

3 Tbsp sugar

Pinch of salt

170 g (5½ oz) natural low-fat or whole-milk yoghurt

Combine butter, flour, cornmeal, sugar, and salt in a food processor and pulse until mixture resembles fine breadcrumbs. Or, in a bowl, work butter into dry ingredients with a pastry blender or 2 dinner knives. Add yoghurt and continue to pulse or stir until mixture starts to come together in a ball. Do not overwork. Turn dough out on to a work surface covered with clingfilm and press into 2 rounds. Chill for at least 20 minutes, or freeze for about 10 minutes.

Note: Dough will keep in refrigerator for up to 5 days or in freezer for up to 3 months.

To prepare: 20 minutes, plus 20 minutes to chill

Enough dough for two 25-cm (10-inch) tarts or twelve 14-cm (5½-inch) tartlets

mango-passion sauce

Put the peeled flesh of 2 ripe mangoes in a blender. Add a little grated peeled fresh ginger, a splash of maple syrup, and a cupful of cold pineapple juice. Purée until smooth. Add a little passion fruit pulp, if available. Serve over sliced pineapple or persimmons.

peach melba

Gently poach peach halves in sugar syrup (made of equal parts water and sugar) until tender. Let cool. Purée fresh or thawed frozen raspberries with a little icing sugar, then strain. Top peaches with a drizzle of raspberry sauce and serve, with vanilla sorbet if desired.

brandied kumquats

Place washed kumquats in a clean jar with two-thirds of their volume of sugar. Add brandy to cover, seal tightly, and store in a cool, dark place for 1 month, turning jar occasionally. Use as a topping for ice cream or yoghurt or a mix-in for fruit salads.

caramel oranges

Gently melt sugar with a splash of water and 1 tsp lemon juice in a saucepan over medium-high heat. Cook without stirring until deep gold. Pour at once over peeled and sliced oranges. If eaten at once, the caramel will break into crunchy shards. The caramel will dissolve on standing.

carrot cupcakes with mascarpone icing

90 g (3 oz) butter at room temperature

185 g (6 oz) granulated sugar

1 Tbsp maple syrup or honey

1 Tbsp finely grated orange zest

2 eggs

125 g (4 oz) grated carrot

155 g (5 oz) plus 2 Tbsp plain flour

2 tsp baking powder

105 ml (3½ fl oz) fresh orange juice, warmed

1 tsp bicarbonate of soda

Mascarpone Icing

90 g (3 oz) butter at room temperature

185 g (6 oz) icing sugar

1 tsp grated lemon zest

125 g (4 oz) chilled mascarpone or low-fat curd or soft cheese

Strips of dried mango for garnish (optional)

Preheat oven to 180°C (350°F). Line a muffin tin with 10 paper liners.

Beat butter, granulated sugar, maple syrup, and orange zest together in a bowl until pale and creamy. Beat in eggs one at a time. Stir in carrot. Sift flour and baking powder together into a bowl. Stir orange juice and bicarbonate of soda together in another small bowl. Stir flour mixture into creamed mixture in 2 additions alternately with orange juice mixture in 2 additions until smooth. Do not overbeat, or cupcakes will be tough.

Spoon batter into prepared muffin tin. Bake until cupcakes are risen and lightly golden, about 20 minutes. Let cupcakes stand for 10 minutes in pan on a wire rack, then turn out onto a baking sheet and let cool completely, about 1 hour.

For Icing: Cream butter and icing sugar together in a bowl until light and fluffy. Stir in lemon zest and mascarpone until blended.

Once cupcakes are cooled, ice them and garnish with strips of dried mango, if desired.

Note: Store cupcakes in an airtight container for up to 3 days.

To prepare: 10 minutes

To cook: 20–25 minutes

10 cupcakes

golden kiwi fruit pavlovas

Meringue(s)

4 egg whites (see Note) at room temperature

Pinch of salt

220 g (7 oz) caster sugar

1 tsp cornflour

½ tsp malt vinegar

1 l (1¾ pints) bottled passion fruit juice (see Notes)

250 ml (8 fl oz) chilled double cream

1–2 Tbsp icing sugar

4 or 5 golden kiwi fruits, peeled and diced

Fresh passion fruit pulp for drizzling (optional)

Choose a baking day that is not humid to make pavlovas. Preheat the oven to 165°C (325°F). Line a baking sheet with non-stick baking paper.

For Meringue(s): In a large bowl, beat egg whites with salt until soft peaks form when the whisk is lifted. Gradually beat in caster sugar and continue to beat until mixture is glossy and very thick and stiff peaks form when whisk is lifted. Beat in cornflour and vinegar.

For individual meringues, use a large spoon to make 6–8 mounds of egg mixture on prepared pan, allowing 2.5–5 cm (1–2 inches) between them. For 1 large meringue, spoon into a single large mound. Swirl top(s) with a fork or icing spatula.

Bake for 2 minutes, then reduce oven temperature to 120°C (250°F). Continue to bake until crisp to the touch, about 1 hour for individual meringues and 1 hour and 40–50 minutes for a large meringue. Turn off oven and leave meringue(s) in oven to cool completely, about 2 hours or up to overnight. Store in an airtight container for up to 1 week.

Boil passion fruit juice in a non-reactive saucepan over medium-high heat until reduced to 160 ml (5 fl oz). Cover and chill thoroughly, at least 2 hours. It must be very cold before adding to cream. In a bowl, whip cream until soft peaks form. Fold in reduced juice and icing sugar. Cover and chill until ready to serve.

To serve, top meringue(s) with flavoured cream and sprinkle with diced kiwi fruit. Drizzle with passion fruit pulp, if using.

Notes: For best results with any kind of meringue, the egg whites should not be too fresh – fresh whites make the mixture "bleed" a clear liquid. If you have access to fresh passion fruit, use it instead of the reduced juice. Simply halve fruit and scoop out seeds, pulp, and juice and fold into whipped cream. Sweeten to taste. If preferred, pulp can be strained to remove seeds.

To prepare: 35 minutes

To cook: 1 hour for individual desserts, 1 hour 40 minutes for a large pavlova; plus 3 hours to cool

6–8 individual pavlovas or 1 large pavlova

lemon soufflés

125 g (4 oz) granulated sugar

125 ml (4 fl oz) lemon juice

Finely grated zest of 1 lemon

½ tsp pure vanilla extract

2 egg whites at room temperature

60 g (2 oz) caster sugar

Icing sugar for dusting

Preheat oven to 375°F (190°C). Combine granulated sugar, lemon juice, and zest in a saucepan and cook over medium heat, stirring occasionally, until sugar is dissolved. Reduce heat to low and simmer for 3 minutes. Remove from heat and stir in vanilla.

In a large bowl, beat egg whites until soft peaks form when the whisk is lifted. Gradually beat in caster sugar and continue to beat until mixture is thick and glossy. Meanwhile, bring lemon mixture back to a boil. While whisking, add 60 ml (2 fl oz) hot lemon mixture into egg whites and beat until very light and fluffy, about 5 minutes.

Divide remaining lemon mixture among six 250-ml (8–fl oz) ramekins (about 2 teaspoons per cup). Divide egg whites among ramekins, making peaks on top with the back of a spoon. Bake until just beginning to brown, 5–6 minutes. Do not overcook, or soufflés will shrink as they cool. Remove from oven, dust with icing sugar, and serve at once.

To prepare: 25 minutes

To cook: 5–6 minutes

6 individual soufflés

sweet potato pie

185 g (6 oz) finely crushed digestive biscuit crumbs or other plain biscuit crumbs

2 tsp ground ginger

125 g (4 oz) butter, melted

Filling

250 g (8 oz) mashed or puréed cooked sweet potato

250 g (8 oz) low-fat sour cream

105 g (3½ oz) soft brown sugar

3 eggs

1 Tbsp dark molasses or black treacle

1 Tbsp grated fresh ginger

1 tsp ground cinnamon

1 tsp ground allspice

Preheat oven to 325°F (165°C). Stir crumbs, ginger, and butter together in a bowl until blended. Press into bottom and sides of a 25-cm (10-inch) loose-bottomed tart or flan tin and chill for 30 minutes.

For Filling: Stir all filling ingredients together in a bowl until evenly blended. Remove chilled crust from refrigerator and press firmly into pan to compact it evenly. Spoon filling into crust. Bake until filling is set and springy to the touch and a skewer inserted in centre comes out clean, about 45 minutes. Transfer pan to a wire rack and let cool. Unmould and chill for at least 1 hour.

Note: Pie will keep for up to 5 days in refrigerator.

To prepare: 30 minutes,
plus 30 minutes to chill

To cook: 45 minutes,
plus 1 hour to chill

8–10 servings

golden fruit bowl with allspice syrup

Allspice Syrup

125 g (4 oz) sugar

12 whole allspice

Zest of ½ orange, in one piece, removed with a vegetable peeler

½ pineapple

2 oranges, peeled and segmented

½ cantaloupe or ogen melon, halved, seeded, and flesh cut into bite-sized chunks

For syrup: Combine sugar and 180 ml (6 fl oz) water in a small, heavy saucepan. Cook over medium heat, stirring until sugar is dissolved. Add allspice and orange zest and simmer gently for 10 minutes. Let cool, then strain through a fine-meshed sieve.

Cut peel from pineapple and trim away eyes. Remove core. Slice horizontally, then cut into bite-sized chunks.

Put pineapple, oranges, and melon into a serving bowl. Pour syrup over fruit and refrigerate for at least 20 minutes or up to 4 hours.

To prepare: 20 minutes, plus 20 minutes to chill

To cook: 10 minutes

8 servings

golden cherry clafoutis

Batter

250 ml (8 fl oz) low-fat or full-cream milk

3 eggs

105 g (3½ oz) plain flour

2 Tbsp granulated sugar

Pinch of salt

2 Tbsp Grand Marnier, Cointreau, or other orange liqueur, or orange juice

Grated zest of ½ orange

1 tsp butter

2 tart apples, cored and thinly sliced

2 Tbsp granulated sugar

125 g (4 oz) golden cherries, stoned if desired

1 Tbsp icing sugar

Preheat oven to 220°C (425°F). Generously butter a shallow 30-cm (12-inch) baking dish.

For batter: Whisk milk, eggs, flour, granulated sugar, and salt together in a bowl until smooth. Stir in liqueur and zest. Strain through a fine-mesh sieve. Batter will be thin.

Melt butter in a frying pan over high heat. Add apple slices and sprinkle with granulated sugar. Sauté until softened, 3–4 minutes. Distribute apple slices evenly in prepared dish. Pour batter over apples and scatter with cherries (they will sink into batter). Bake until brown and lightly puffed, 30–35 minutes. Dust with icing sugar and serve at once.

Variation: Use 125 g (4 oz) fresh berries, such as blueberries, raspberries, or blackberries, instead of cherries. Do not use Bramleys for the tart apples as they will fall to pieces; try Granny Smiths or Newtowns.

To prepare: 35 minutes

To cook: 30–35 minutes

6 servings

cherries strawberries red plums

RED FRUITS AND VEGETABLES PROVIDE ANTIOXIDANTS

pomegranates ruby grapefruits

FOR PROTECTION AND HEALING • PROMOTE HEART

rhubarb cranberries red grapes

HEALTH • PROMOTE URINARY TRACT HEALTH • HELP

watermelons red apples quinces

REDUCE THE RISK OF CERTAIN CANCERS • IMPROVE

raspberries pink grapefruits red

MEMORY FUNCTION • RED FRUITS AND VEGETABLES

pears pomegranates red plums

OFFER ANTIOXIDANTS FOR PROTECTION AND HEALING

Red

Red is the colour of ripeness, the deepest hue that many fruits reach after passing through stages of green or yellow. To take advantage of these fruits' colourful phytonutrients – some of which they share with blue fruits, at the other end of the colour spectrum – leave them unpeeled whenever possible. You'll also reap the benefits of the extra fibre that the skin contains.

Red fruits are usually hard to find in the chilly weeks of early spring, since they need long, hot, sunny days to develop their full colour. Strawberries, however, are at their jewel-like best at this time of year. Enjoy ripe strawberries adorned with only a sprinkle of sugar or a splash of cream, or with a drizzle of sweet balsamic vinegar for a greater flavour contrast (page 101). Or combine them with smooth, mild, naturally low-fat ricotta cheese in an updated English trifle (page 95). Summertime brings more red berries and cherries, fruits best enjoyed in their brief natural season. Cherries are delicious simmered into a rich-tasting filling for lacy crêpes (page 102).

Other red fruits come into their own in autumn and winter. Less common fruits make an appearance at this time of year: pomegranates, with their hundreds of translucent ruby seeds, and quinces, which appear yellow-orange when raw but actually develop red-hued phytochemicals as they cook, changing colour from pink to ruby red.

SPRING	SUMMER	AUTUMN	WINTER
pink or ruby grapefruit	cherries	red apples	red apples
blood oranges	red grapes	cranberries	cranberries
red pears	red plums	red grapes	pink or ruby grapefruit
rhubarb	raspberries	red pears	red grapes
strawberries	rhubarb	red plums	blood oranges
	strawberries	pomegranates	red pears
	watermelon	quinces	pomegranates
		raspberries	quinces
		rhubarb	
		watermelon	

berry & ricotta trifles

315 g (10 oz) raspberry or blackcurrant jam

60 ml (2 fl oz) kirsch or sherry

60 ml (2 fl oz) orange juice

375 g (12 oz) ricotta cheese

30 g (1 oz) icing sugar

1 tsp pure vanilla extract

1 sponge cake, purchased or homemade (*below*), 18 cm (7 inches) in diameter, cut into 2.5-cm (1-inch) cubes

450 g (1 lb) strawberries, cored and sliced

If desired, push raspberry jam through a sieve with back of a large spoon to remove seeds. Stir jam, kirsch, and orange juice together in a small bowl. Purée ricotta, sugar, and vanilla in a blender until smooth.

Divide half the cake cubes among 6 serving glasses. Drizzle one-third of jam mixture evenly over sponge cake. Top with one-third of strawberries, then half of ricotta mixture. Repeat with layers of sponge cake, jam mixture, berries, and ricotta. Top with a final layer of strawberries and spoon the remaining third of jam mixture over all.

Cover and chill for at least 1 hour before serving.

Note: Trifles can be covered and stored for up to 12 hours in refrigerator.

To prepare: 20 minutes, plus 1 hour to chill

6 servings

sponge cake

3 eggs at room temperature

155 g (5 oz) caster sugar

Pinch of salt

90 g (3 oz) cake flour

30 g (1 oz) cornflour

1 tsp baking powder

3 Tbsp butter, melted and cooled

Preheat oven to 180°C (350°F). Line an 18-cm (7-inch) cake tin with non-stick baking paper to cover bottom and sides.

Using an electric mixer on high speed, beat eggs, sugar, and salt together until they reach a thick, creamy ribbonlike texture, about 15 minutes. Sift flour, cornflour, and baking powder together. Using a large slotted spoon, gently fold dry ingredients into egg mixture, one-third at a time. Gently fold in butter.

Pour batter into prepared tin and bake until cake springs back when lightly pressed, 30–35 minutes. Remove from oven and let cool in pan on a wire rack. Turn out and wrap in clingfilm when completely cool.

Note: Sponge cake will keep in the refrigerator for 5 days or can be frozen for up to 2 months.

To prepare: 30 minutes

To cook: 30 minutes, plus 40 minutes to cool

One 18-cm (7-inch) cake, 6–8 servings

plum cake

Vegetable oil spray

235 g (7½ oz) plain flour

1 teaspoon baking powder

¼ teaspoon salt

250 g (8 oz) butter at room temperature

250 g (8 oz) plus 1 Tbsp sugar

2 large eggs at room temperature

6–8 plums (about 450 g/1 lb), halved, stoned, each half cut into 4 slices

¼ teaspoon ground cinnamon

Place a rack in lower third of oven and preheat to 180°C (350°F). Coat a 23-cm (9-inch) round or 20-cm (8-inch) square cake tin with vegetable oil spray. Line bottom with non-stick baking paper and coat paper with more spray.

Whisk together flour, baking powder, and salt. Using an electric mixer, beat together butter and 250 g (8 oz) sugar until pale and fluffy. Add eggs one at a time, beating well after each addition. Add flour mixture and mix well.

Pour batter into prepared pan and spread evenly. Poke plum slices into the batter, placing them close together. In a small bowl, combine cinnamon and 1 Tbsp sugar, and sprinkle over surface.

Bake until top is golden, edges pull away from pan, and a skewer inserted in centre comes out clean, 50–60 minutes. Let cool for about 30 minutes before serving.

Note: Other stone fruits can be used in place of the plums, such as apricots, nectarines, and peaches. Store cake in an airtight container in the refrigerator for up to 3 days or freeze for up to 2 months.

To prepare: 30 minutes

To cook: 50 minutes, plus 30 minutes to cool

8 servings

raspberry jellies

1 Tbsp (1 envelope) unflavoured powdered gelatine

750 ml (24 fl oz) cranberry juice or grape juice, chilled

375 g (12 oz) raspberries or seedless red grapes

In a cup or small bowl, sprinkle gelatine over 60 ml (2 fl oz) water and let stand until absorbed, about 3 minutes. Heat in microwave for about 20 seconds or in a small saucepan over low heat on hob for about 1 minute to dissolve. Stir well to ensure that gelatine is fully dissolved. In a bowl, combine gelatine and 250 ml (8 fl oz) juice and mix well. Chill for 20 minutes. Add remaining 500 ml (16 fl oz) juice, stirring to blend well. Divide raspberries among six 250-ml (8–fl oz) serving glasses or bowls. Pour juice mixture over fruit. Cover with clingfilm and chill until fully set, about 4 hours or up to 2 days.

Note: Sparkling grape or apple juice and green grapes can also be used for these jellies.

To prepare: 30 minutes, plus 4 hours to set

6 servings

cherries flambéed in rum

155 g (5 oz) redcurrant or
raspberry jam

3 Tbsp sugar

1 Tbsp lemon juice

450 g (1 lb) fresh cherries, stemmed
and stoned if desired (see Note)

80 ml (3 fl oz) rum or kirsch

Crème fraîche for serving

Push jam through a fine-mesh sieve with back of a large spoon to remove seeds. Combine jam, sugar, 125 ml (4 fl oz) water, and lemon juice in a large, heavy, non-reactive saucepan. Simmer over medium heat until slightly syrupy, 2–3 minutes. Add cherries and simmer until slightly softened, 2–3 minutes more. Add a little water if mixture starts to caramelise. Divide hot fruit among serving glasses and spoon syrup over it. Heat rum in a microwave for 20 seconds or in a small saucepan over low heat for 1–2 minutes. Away from open flame, pour rum over fruit and carefully ignite fumes with a long match. Serve with crème fraîche.

Note: The cherries look prettier with their stems attached but will be easier to eat if they are stoned. This recipe is also a great way to prepare peeled, fresh peach halves, in which case use apricot jam.

To prepare: 15 minutes

To cook: 10 minutes

4 servings

rhubarb fool

315 g (10 oz) 12-mm (½-inch) lengths
rhubarb (8 or 9 stalks)

185 g (6 oz) granulated sugar, plus
more if needed

375 ml (12 fl oz) double cream

1½ Tbsp icing sugar

1 Tbsp kirsch or raspberry brandy
(optional)

In a saucepan, combine rhubarb, 160 ml (5 fl oz) water, and granulated sugar. Cover and cook over low heat, stirring occasionally, until rhubarb is tender and breaks up easily, about 8 minutes. Purée in a food processor or blender. Taste and add more sugar if needed. Cover and chill for at least 1 hour or for up to 3 days.

In a deep bowl, whip cream with icing sugar until soft peaks form when the whisk is lifted. Stir in kirsch, if using. Spoon cream and rhubarb purée into martini glasses or tall serving glasses in alternate layers, swirling a fork gently through layers to combine them slightly. Chill for at least 30 minutes before serving.

Note: Other acidic fruit purées, such as plum, gooseberry, and raspberry, can be used in place of rhubarb.

*To prepare: 20 minutes,
plus 1½ hours to chill*

To cook: 8 minutes

5 or 6 servings

biscuit & berry "tartlets"

Biscuits make a great dessert base for fresh berries. Spread shortbread or other thin, crisp biscuits with a little jam and arrange fresh raspberries in a circular pattern on top. Serve with raspberry purée or sauce if desired.

slow-baked quinces

Put whole or halved peeled quinces in a baking dish and add a generous splash of red wine and a liberal sprinkling of sugar. Cover and bake in a 165°C (325°F) oven for about 4 hours, topping up the liquid from time-to-time as needed.

strawberries with balsamic vinegar

Balsamic vinegar is a delicious and surprising complement to strawberries. Choose an aged true balsamic and the smallest, ripest red berries you can find. Drizzle the strawberries with balsamic and sprinkle with black pepper.

mixed berry compote

Simmer fresh or frozen raspberries or a mixture of berries with a couple of bay leaves, a cinnamon stick, a vanilla bean, and sugar to taste. Cook gently until slightly syrupy, about 30 minutes. Add a little lemon juice.

brandied berry crêpes

Crêpe Batter
105 g (3½ oz) plain flour

1 Tbsp sugar

¼ tsp salt

250 ml (8 fl oz) chilled low-fat or full-cream milk

1 egg

1 egg yolk

2 Tbsp butter, melted

1 tsp pure vanilla extract

2 Tbsp butter, or as needed

Filling
250 g (8 oz) raspberries

60 g (2 oz) sugar

1 Tbsp cornflour mixed with 60 ml (2 fl oz) brandy

1 Tbsp lemon juice

250 g (8 oz) mixed fresh red berries, such as stoned cherries, stemmed redcurrants, cranberries, and cored and sliced strawberries

For Batter: Whisk all batter ingredients together in a bowl until smooth. Strain through a fine-meshed sieve to remove any lumps. Let stand for at least 15 minutes, or cover and refrigerate for up to 8 hours.

Melt a little of the 2 Tbsp butter in a crêpe pan, omelette pan, or small frying pan over medium-high heat and cook until butter smells nutty and just starts to brown. Pour in a small ladleful (3 Tbsp) of batter and quickly tilt pan to coat bottom evenly. Cook just until batter is set and golden on bottom, then flip and cook on second side for another minute or two. Repeat to make 8 crêpes, brushing pan with more butter as needed. Stack cooked crêpes on a plate. If not using at once, let cool, cover with clingfilm, and let stand for up to 2 hours or refrigerate for up to 12 hours.

For Filling: Combine raspberries and sugar in a non-reactive saucepan and cook over medium heat, stirring, until sugar is dissolved. Reduce heat to maintain a simmer, stir in brandy mixture, and cook, stirring, until slightly thickened. Stir in lemon juice. Strain through a fine-meshed sieve. If not serving crêpes at once, let sauce cool, cover and refrigerate for up to 5 days.

To serve, bring sauce to a simmer and add mixed fruits. Return to a simmer, then remove from heat. Reheat crêpes in microwave oven for 30 seconds or in low 95°C (200°F) oven covered with foil for 10 minutes. (If crêpes have been chilled, reheat for 1 minute in microwave oven or 15 minutes in 180°C/350°F oven.)

Spoon filling into each crêpe and fold into quarters. Serve at once.

To prepare: 30 minutes

To cook: 15 minutes

8 filled crepes, 4 servings

pear & frangipane galettes

½ recipe Pastry Case (page 34)

2 Tbsp butter

3 red-skinned pears, cored and diced

1 Tbsp sugar

Frangipane Filling

155 g (5 oz) ground almonds

90 g (3 oz) butter, softened

90 g (3 oz) sugar

1 tsp kirsch (optional)

¼ tsp almond extract

1 egg

Thyme sprigs for garnish (optional)

Roll out pastry on a lightly floured work surface to 3 mm (⅛ inch) thick. Cut out six 13-cm (5-inch) rounds, re-rolling pastry as needed. Place rounds on a baking sheet lined with non-stick baking paper, allowing a little space between them, and chill until ready to bake.

Preheat oven to 180°C (350°F). Melt butter in a heavy frying pan over medium-high heat and cook until it bubbles and starts to brown. Add pears and sugar and cook, tossing frequently, until lightly browned, about 1–2 minutes. Let cool.

For Filling: Whisk all filling ingredients together in a bowl until evenly combined. Spread 2 Tbsp filling on each pastry round, leaving a 12-mm (½-inch) margin around edge. Top each with the cooled pears, dividing evenly. Crimp pastry edges. Bake until golden and cooked through, about 30 minutes. Garnish with thyme sprigs, if desired, and serve.

To prepare: 10 minutes

To cook: 30 minutes

6 servings

raspberries in red wine syrup

250 ml (8 fl oz) dry red wine, such as Merlot

125 ml (4 fl oz) port

185 g (6 oz) sugar

6 whole cloves

1 cinnamon stick

6 cardamom pods

375 g (12 oz) raspberries

2 tsp best-quality unsweetened cocoa powder (optional)

Combine all ingredients except the raspberries and cocoa in a saucepan. Bring to a simmer over medium heat, stirring until sugar is dissolved. Reduce heat to low and simmer until syrupy and reduced by half, 20–25 minutes. Let cool slightly or completely.

Spoon syrup on to serving plates and top with a mound of raspberries. Dust with cocoa powder, if desired.

Note: The syrup can be made in quantity and refrigerated in a covered container for up to 4 weeks. It is also excellent with fresh figs.

To prepare: 5 minutes

To cook: 20–25 minutes

4 servings

ruby grapefruit sorbet

2 tsp unflavoured powdered gelatine

250 g (8 oz) sugar

60 ml (2 fl oz) lemon juice, strained

625 ml (1 pint) ruby grapefruit juice

60 ml (2 fl oz) orange juice

2 egg whites

In a cup, sprinkle gelatine over 60 ml (2 fl oz) cold water and let stand until absorbed, about 3 minutes. Combine sugar and 125 ml (4 fl oz) cold water in a non-reactive saucepan and simmer for 5 minutes, stirring, until sugar is dissolved. Remove from heat and stir in gelatine mixture until dissolved. Let cool, then stir in fruit juices. Pour into a shallow metal baking tin and freeze until mixture begins to solidify, about 2 hours. Transfer to a food processor or bowl and pulse, or beat with an electric mixer or whisk, to break up. Add egg whites and continue pulsing or beating until light and fluffy. Cover and freeze until firm, at least 4 hours. If frozen for more than 48 hours before using, beat again, then refreeze for 4 hours for best consistency.

To prepare: 30 minutes, plus 6 hours to freeze

To cook: 5 minutes

About 1 quart, 6–8 servings

redcurrant filo tarts

6 sheets thawed frozen filo dough, about 50 x 30 cm (20 x 12 inches) each

60 g (2 oz) butter, melted

60 g (2 oz) granulated sugar

2 Tbsp redcurrant or raspberry jam or jelly

250 g (8 oz) stemmed fresh redcurrants, raspberries, or hulled and sliced strawberries

1 Tbsp icing sugar

Preheat oven to 165°C (325°F). Lay a sheet of filo on a baking sheet; keep remaining filo covered with a towel. Brush filo sheet with a little butter and sprinkle with a little granulated sugar. Top with another sheet, brush with butter, and sprinkle with sugar. Repeat with remaining filo, stacking layers and ending with a brushing of butter only. Press the filo stack firmly and evenly to compact layers. Using a sharp knife, cut out six 13-cm (5-inch) rounds. Butter six 10-cm (4-inch) tart tins and press a filo round into each. Sprinkle with remaining granulated sugar.

Bake until crisp and golden, about 20 minutes. Transfer tins to wire racks and let cool to the touch. Remove filo shells from tins and let cool completely on wire racks. Use at once or store in an airtight container at room temperature for up to 5 days. Crisp in a warm oven for 5–10 minutes, if necessary.

Up to an hour before serving, whisk jam or jelly in a bowl to soften. Add berries and stir gently to combine. Spoon into filo shells. Dust with icing sugar just before serving.

To prepare: 15 minutes

To cook: 20 minutes

6 servings

cashews pistachio nuts polenta

WHOLE GRAINS, PULSES, SEEDS, AND NUTS PROMOTE

coffee macadamia nuts pecans

ARTERY AND HEART HEALTH • HELP REDUCE THE RISK

almonds peanuts whole wheat

OF DIABETES • REDUCE HIGH BLOOD PRESSURE • OFFER

oats chestnuts dark chocolate

ANTIOXIDANTS FOR PROTECTION AND HEALING • HELP

hazelnuts pine nuts brown rice

REDUCE THE RISK OF STROKE • MAY REDUCE THE RISK

walnuts cashews pistachio nuts

OF CANCERS OF THE BREAST, PROSTATE AND COLON

Brown

This down-to-earth chapter of the healthy-eating rainbow is devoted not to fruits or vegetables, but to a distinctive group of healthy foods that come from plants: grains and seeds. Nuts are a type of seed that lend themselves well to sweet preparations. Two particular seeds – the coffee bean and the cocoa bean – are unique in their antioxidant benefits and widespread appeal, bordering on obsession.

Grains might not leap to mind when you think about dessert, but they can play a number of roles in the final course of the meal. Rolled oats make a crunchy streusel topping for fruit crisps (page 123) and stone-ground cornmeal adds texture to a rustic polenta cake (page 124) and a golden, sweet pastry crust (page 79).

Coffee and chocolate are currently being studied for their rich phytochemical content and beneficial effects against a range of ailments. Unless you are particularly sensitive to caffeine, you needn't feel that a coffee or chocolate dessert is a guilty pleasure. On a summer evening, an espresso granita (page 119) combines dessert and coffee into one simple and refreshing ending to a meal.

Nuts, a highly nutritious member of the brown group, are marvellous additions to a number of sweet dishes. Rice pudding with pistachios (page 120) and hazelnut-dotted Prune Panforte (page 113) are especially good made with freshly picked nuts.

GRAINS	PULSES	NUTS	OTHER
oats	peanuts	almonds	coffee
polenta (corn)		Brazil nuts	dark chocolate
brown rice		cashews	
whole wheat		chestnuts	
		hazelnuts	
		macadamia nuts	
		pecans	
		pine nuts	
		pistachio nuts	
		walnuts	

prune panforte

170 g (5½ oz) almonds

155 g (5 oz) hazelnuts

375 g (12 oz) stoned prunes or mixed prunes and dried figs, diced

125 g (4 oz) plain flour

2 Tbsp unsweetened cocoa powder

2 tsp ground cinnamon

1 tsp ground allspice

¼ tsp freshly grated nutmeg

1 tsp ground ginger

185 g (6 oz) honey

125 g (4 oz) granulated sugar

60 g (2 oz) plain chocolate, chopped

Icing sugar for dusting

Preheat oven to 150°C (300°F). Butter a 23-cm (9-inch) springform tin and line bottom with non-stick baking paper. Spread almonds and hazelnuts on baking sheets and toast for 20 minutes, shaking the pans every 5 minutes. Pour hazelnuts into a clean kitchen towel and rub together to remove skins. Coarsely chop almonds and halve hazelnuts. Stir nuts, dried fruit, flour, cocoa powder, and spices together in a bowl.

Heat honey and granulated sugar in a saucepan over medium-high heat until sugar is dissolved, then boil to 112°C (234°F) on a sugar thermometer or until a small amount of mixture dropped into very cold water forms a soft ball that flattens when removed from water. Remove from heat, add chocolate and stir until smooth. Pour into nut mixture and quickly stir with a sturdy wooden spoon until combined. Work quickly, as mixture thickens fast. Press into prepared tin and bake until set, about 35 minutes. Let cool slightly in tin on a wire rack, but remove from tin while still warm and let cool completely on rack. Dust with icing sugar and cut into thin slices to serve.

Note: Store in an airtight container for 3–4 weeks.

To prepare: 25 minutes

To cook: 35 minutes, plus 2 hours to cool

20 servings

brazil nut & almond torte

90 g (3 oz) finely crushed digestive biscuits or other plain biscuit crumbs

315 g (10 oz) sugar

2 tsp baking powder

155 g (5 oz) Brazil nuts, finely chopped

125 g (4 oz) flaked almonds, finely chopped

185 g (6 oz) stoned dates, finely chopped

90 g (3 oz) plain chocolate, finely chopped, or 90 g (3 oz) chocolate chips

8 egg whites

Preheat oven to 165°C (325°F). Butter a 23-cm (9-inch) springform tin and line bottom with non-stick baking paper. Sprinkle the paper with biscuit crumbs. Stir sugar and baking powder together in a bowl. Add nuts and dates. Break up dates with your fingertips so they are evenly distributed. Stir in chocolate.

In a large bowl, beat egg whites until stiff, glossy peaks form when the whisk is lifted. Fold in nut mixture until evenly blended. Spoon into prepared tin and smooth top. Bake until firm to the touch, about 1½ hours. Let cool completely in tin on a wire rack for at least 2 hours.

Unlatch tin sides and transfer cake to a plate. Cut into wedges to serve.

Note: Store left-over cake wrapped tightly in foil in an airtight container at room temperature for several weeks.

To prepare: 45 minutes

To cook: 1½ hours, plus 2 hours to cool

16 servings

almond cake
with kirsch syrup

315 g (10 oz) sugar

6 large eggs, separated

Finely grated zest of 1 lemon

Finely grated zest of ½ orange

155 g (5 oz) ground almonds

75 g (2½ oz) plain flour

1 tsp baking powder

1 tsp almond extract

Kirsch Syrup

3 Tbsp kirsch

1 Tbsp lemon juice

2 Tbsp sugar

Preheat oven to 165°C (325°F). Butter a 23-cm (9-inch) springform tin and line bottom with non-stick baking paper.

Beat sugar, egg yolks, and zests together in a large bowl with an electric mixer until thick and pale, about 10 minutes. Stir almonds, flour, and baking powder together in a small bowl. Add to egg yolk mixture with almond extract and stir to blend.

In a deep metal bowl, beat egg whites until soft peaks form when the whisk is lifted. Gently fold whites into egg yolk mixture. Pour into prepared tin and carefully smooth top without deflating batter. Bake until cake springs back when lightly touched, 60–65 minutes. Unlatch sides of tin and transfer cake onto a wire rack while hot.

For Kirsch Syrup: Combine kirsch, lemon juice, and sugar in a small non-reactive saucepan. Cook over medium heat, stirring until sugar is dissolved. Remove from heat and brush hot syrup gently and evenly over cake. Let cool completely before serving.

Notes: Serve with stoned fresh raspberries or cherries and crème fraîche, or split in half horizontally and fill with chopped fresh fruit folded into a little whipped chilled cream. Store cake in a covered container at room temperature for up to 5 days.

To prepare: 20 minutes

To cook: 1 hour

10–12 servings

hazelnut macaroons

155 g (5 oz) hazelnuts

5 egg whites at room temperature

Pinch of salt

220 g (7 oz) caster sugar

185 g (6 oz) icing sugar, sifted

1 tsp baking powder

1 tsp pure vanilla extract

Choose a baking day that is not humid to make macaroons. Preheat oven to 165°C (325°F). Spread hazelnuts in a single layer on a baking sheet. Toast for 20 minutes, shaking pan every 5 minutes. Pour nuts into a clean kitchen towel and rub together to remove skins. Let cool completely, then chop finely with a chef's knife (do not do this in a food processor, or nuts will release too much oil and become pasty). Leave oven on.

In a large bowl, beat egg whites with salt until soft peaks form when the whisk is lifted. Gradually beat in caster sugar until stiff, glossy peaks form. Stir icing sugar and baking powder together in a bowl until blended. Fold into egg whites with vanilla, then fold in cooled nuts with a metal spoon. Do not beat, or oils in nuts will deflate the mixture.

Line baking sheets with non-stick baking paper. Place teaspoonfuls of batter on prepared pans, allowing a little space between them. Place pans in oven and immediately lower oven temperature to 120°C (250°F). Bake until macaroons are dry and crisp, about 1 hour. Turn off oven and leave macaroons in oven to cool completely, about 2 hours or up to overnight.

Note: If you like, dip macaroons in melted chocolate and sprinkle with chopped hazelnuts, or serve with fresh raspberries and raspberry sauce (see page 80).

To prepare: 45 minutes

To cook: 1 hour, plus 2 hours to cool

About 60 macaroons

real hot chocolate

500 ml (16 fl oz) low-fat or full-cream milk

75 g (2½ oz) best-quality dark chocolate, finely chopped

1½ Tbsp sugar

1 cinnamon stick

1–2 Tbsp Kahlúa or other coffee liqueur (optional)

In a saucepan, combine milk, chocolate, sugar, and cinnamon stick. Warm over low heat, stirring to dissolve sugar, until bubbles form around edges of pan. Discard cinnamon stick and whisk mixture until frothy. Whisk in Kahlúa, if using. Pour into cups and serve at once.

To prepare: 10 minutes

To cook: 5 minutes

2 servings

chocolate-dipped strawberries

Chop dark chocolate into small pieces and melt in a saucepan over low heat. Dip strawberries in melted chocolate to coat three-quarters of each fruit. Place on non-stick baking paper to set. Serve on same day.

affogato

For this Italian favourite combining ice cream and hot coffee, put a scoop of vanilla ice cream in a heat-proof tumbler and garnish with broken praline, if you like. Serve a small cup of espresso with it for diners to pour over the ice cream.

caramelised hazelnuts & harvest fruits

Sauté sliced pears and apples in a little butter and brown sugar until they start to caramelise. Mix in generous handfuls toasted hazelnuts and almonds and chopped dates. Serve with a dollop of crème fraîche, if desired.

espresso granita

Pour 500 ml (16 fl oz) strong, sweetened coffee into a shallow metal pan and freeze until slushy, stirring occasionally. Draw a fork through mixture when it is frozen to break it up into icy crystals. Scoop into serving glasses.

chocolate-pumpkin cake

250 g (8 oz) granulated sugar

1 egg

125 ml (4 fl oz) low-fat or full-cream milk
or natural yoghurt

125 g (4 oz) shredded raw pumpkin
(see Note)

30 g (1 oz) best-quality unsweetened
cocoa powder

90 g (3 oz) chocolate chips

125 g (4 oz) butter, softened

1 tsp bicarbonate of soda

1 tsp pure vanilla extract

250 g (8 oz) soft-wheat flour

2 tsp baking powder

125 ml (4 fl oz) strong, hot coffee

Icing sugar for dusting

Preheat oven to 165°C (325°F). Butter a 23-cm (9-inch) diameter round cake tin and line bottom with non-stick baking paper.

Combine all ingredients except icing sugar in a food processor and process to blend, 30–40 seconds, or beat in a bowl with an electric mixer or by hand. Pour into prepared tin and smooth top.

Bake until cake has risen and set and a skewer inserted in centre comes out clean, about 50 minutes. Let cool in tin on a wire rack. Remove from tin and dust with icing sugar. Cut into wedges to serve.

Note: The magic ingredient in this cake is grated raw pumpkin. Its colour and flavour are indiscernible in the baked cake but it creates a moist texture. If preferred, the same amount of shredded carrot can be used instead of pumpkin. Store cake in a sealed container at room temperature for up to a week.

To prepare: 15 minutes

To cook: 50 minutes

8–10 servings

pistachio rice pudding

1.25 l (2 pints) low-fat or full-cream milk

125 ml (4 fl oz) sweetened condensed milk

220 g (7 oz) short-grain rice,
preferably organic

½ tsp ground cardamom

1 tsp pure vanilla extract

90 g (3 oz) dried apricots, chopped

Grated zest of ½ lemon

2 Tbsp double cream (optional)

60 g (2 oz) pistachios, chopped

Combine milk, condensed milk, and rice in a saucepan and bring to a boil over medium heat. Reduce heat to maintain a low simmer and cook, stirring occasionally, for 10 minutes. Add cardamom, vanilla, and two-thirds of the apricots and cook until rice is tender, stirring occasionally, about 10 minutes. Stir in lemon zest and cream, if using.

Serve warm or cold, garnished with pistachios and remaining apricots. To serve cold, press clingfilm directly onto surface to prevent a skin from forming and chill for at least 3–4 hours or up to 24 hours. The pudding will thicken on cooling.

To prepare: 15 minutes

To cook: 20 minutes

6 servings

oatmeal pear crisp

5 firm, just-ripe pears

1 Tbsp granulated sugar

2 tsp cornflour

2 Tbsp lemon juice

105 g (3½ oz) brown sugar

90 g (3 oz) rolled oats

30 g (1 oz) oat bran

105 g (3½ oz) plain flour

1 tsp baking powder

½ tsp cardamom seeds, finely ground

105 g (3½ oz) butter

Yoghurt or crème fraîche for serving

Preheat oven to 180°C (350°F). Quarter, core, and thinly slice pears. Sprinkle with granulated sugar and cornflour and toss gently. Spread slices in an even layer in a shallow baking dish 30 cm (12 inches) in diameter. Sprinkle with lemon juice.

Stir brown sugar, oats, oat bran, flour, baking powder, and cardamom together in a bowl. Finely chop butter and rub into oat mixture with your fingertips until mixture is crumbly, or process mixture in a food processor until crumbly. Sprinkle evenly over fruit. Bake until golden and crisp, about 40 minutes. Serve hot or warm, scooped into bowls and topped with a dollop of yoghurt or crème fraîche.

Note: If cardamom seeds are unavailable, but green pods are, you will need to open 2 pods to get ½ tsp seeds. Oat bran is available at healthfood shops.

To prepare: 15 minutes

To cook: 40 minutes

6 servings

bread pudding

500 ml (16 fl oz) low-fat or full-cream milk

3 eggs

60 g (2 oz) sugar

½ tsp freshly grated nutmeg

2 tsp pure vanilla extract

2 Tbsp butter, softened

7 slices bread, preferably wholemeal

1 large or 2 small tart apples, peeled, cored, and thinly sliced

60 g (2 oz) raisins

30 g (1 oz) flaked almonds

Whisk milk, eggs, sugar, nutmeg, and vanilla together in a bowl until blended. Coat a shallow 30-cm (12-inch) diameter round baking dish with a little butter. Remove crusts from bread and spread bread lightly with remaining butter. Cut each slice into 4 triangles. Interweave bread triangles with apple slices in a single layer in prepared dish. Sprinkle with raisins and almonds. Pour egg mixture into dish. Let stand at room temperature for 15 minutes or refrigerate for up to 4 hours.

Preheat oven to 350°F (180°C). Bake pudding until puffed and golden, about 40 minutes. Serve hot or at room temperature.

Note: You can also bake mixture in four to six 375-ml (12–fl oz) ramekins for 25–30 minutes. Do not use Bramley apples, as they will not hold their shape when cooked.

To prepare: 30 minutes, plus 15 minutes to stand

To cook: 40 minutes

5 or 6 servings

walnut & date tart

185 g (6 oz) stoned dates, chopped

250 ml (8 fl oz) orange juice

155 ml (5 fl oz) golden syrup

2 eggs, lightly beaten

125 g (4 oz) low-fat sour cream

2 tsp cornflour

1 partially baked 25-cm (10-inch) Pastry Case (page 34)

125 g (4 oz) walnut or pecan halves

Sliced pears and whipped cream for serving (optional)

Preheat oven to 180°C (350°F). Combine dates and orange juice in a saucepan and simmer over low heat until dates are soft and pulpy, about 5 minutes. Remove from heat and whisk in syrup and eggs. Stir sour cream and cornflour together in a small bowl and whisk into date mixture. Pour into pastry case and sprinkle with nuts. Bake until filling has set in centre, about 1 hour.

Let cool in pan on a wire rack, then chill for at least 1 hour. Unmould and cut into slender wedges. Serve wedges with pears and whipped cream, if desired.

Note: This filling can also be used for tartlets. Use 8 partially baked 11.5-cm (4½-inch) pastry cases and bake for 35–40 minutes.

To prepare: 15 minutes, plus 1 hour for pastry case

To cook: 1 hour, plus 1 hour to chill

10–12 servings

polenta cake

375 g (12 oz) granulated sugar

2 eggs

Grated zest and juice of 2 lemons

250 ml (8 fl oz) rapeseed oil

185 ml (6 fl oz) low-fat yoghurt

235 g (7½ oz) plain flour

2 tsp baking powder

220 g (7 oz) instant polenta

250 g (8 oz) fresh or frozen blackberries, plus fresh blackberries for garnish (optional)

Icing sugar for dusting

Crème fraîche for serving

Preheat oven to 165°C (325°F). Butter a 23-cm (9-inch) springform tin and line bottom with non-stick baking paper.

Whisk together granulated sugar, eggs, lemon zest and juice, oil, and yoghurt in a bowl. In another bowl, stir flour, baking powder, and polenta together. Gradually stir dry ingredients into wet ingredients until just combined. Fold in blackberries. Pour into prepared pan and smooth top. Bake until springy to touch, about 1½ hours.

Let cool in pan on a wire rack before unlatching sides of tin and transferring cake to a serving plate. Dust with icing sugar and cut into wedges to serve, accompanied with crème fraîche and berries, if using.

Note: Store cake in a covered container in refrigerator for up to 5 days.

To prepare: 10 minutes

To cook: 1½ hours

16 servings

Nutrients at work

Humans need more than forty nutrients to support life. Many foods are good sources of many different nutrients, but no single food provides everything. Eating a variety of foods, preferably in their whole form, is the best way to get all the nutrients your body needs. Some nutrients require others for optimal absorption but excessive amounts may result in heath problems.

Until recently, nutritionists recommended the distribution of carbohydrates, protein, and fat in a well-balanced diet to be 55 per cent of calories from carbohydrates, 15 per cent of calories from protein, and 30 per cent of calories from fat. As we have learned more about individual health needs and

differences in metabolism, we have become more flexible in determining what constitutes a healthy diet. The table below shows macro-nutrient ranges recommended by the Institute of Medicine, part of the U.S. National Academies. These ranges are more likely to accommodate everyone's health needs.

To help you evaluate and balance your diet as you prepare the recipes in this book, turn to pages 130–33 for nutritional analyses of each recipe.

Nutrition experts have also determined guidelines for vitamins and minerals. For more information, see pages 128–29.

CARBOHYDRATES, PROTEIN, AND FATS

NUTRIENTS AND FOOD SOURCES	FUNCTIONS	RECOMMENDED % OF DAILY CALORIES AND GUIDANCE
Carbohydrates COMPLEX CARBOHYDRATES • Grains, breads, cereals, pastas • Dried beans and peas, lentils • Starchy vegetables (potatoes, corn, green peas)	• Main source of energy for the body • Particularly important for the brain and nervous system • Fibre aids normal digestion	45–65% • Favour complex carbohydrates, especially pulses, vegetables, and whole grains (brown rice, wholewheat bread, pasta, and cereal). • Many foods high in complex carbohydrates are also good fibre sources. Among the best are bran cereals, canned and dried beans, dried fruit and oats. Recommended daily intake of fibre for adults under 50 is 25 g for women and 38 g for men. For women over 50, intake is 21 g; for men, 30 g.
SIMPLE CARBOHYDRATES • Naturally occurring sugars in fruits, vegetables, and milk • Added refined sugars in soft drinks, sweets, baked goods, jams and jellies, etc.	• Provide energy	• Fruit and vegetables have naturally occurring sugars but also have vitamins, minerals, and phytochemicals. Refined sugar, on the other hand, has little to offer in the way of nutrition, so limit your intake to get the most from your daily calories.

Source: Institute of Medicine. Dietary Reference Intakes for Energy, Carbohydrates, Fibre, Fat, Protein and Amino Acids (Macronutrients).

NUTRIENTS AND FOOD SOURCES	FUNCTIONS	RECOMMENDED % OF DAILY CALORIES AND GUIDANCE
Protein • Foods from animal sources • Dried beans and peas, nuts • Grain products	• Builds and repairs cells • Regulates body processes by providing components for enzymes, hormones, fluid balance, nerve transmission	10–35% • Choose lean sources such as dried beans, fish, poultry, lean cuts of meat, soy and low-fat dairy foods most of the time. • Egg yolks are rich in many nutrients but also high in cholesterol; limit to 5 per week.
Fats All fats are mixtures of saturated and unsaturated (polyunsaturated and mono-unsaturated) types. Polyunsaturated and especially monounsaturated types are considered more desirable because they promote cardiovascular health.	• Supplies essential fatty acids needed for various body processes and to build cell membranes, particularly of the brain and nervous system • Transports certain vitamins	20–35% • Experts disagree about the ideal amount of total fat in the diet. Some say more is fine if it is heart-healthy fat; others recommend limiting total fat. Virtually all experts agree that saturated fat, trans fats, and cholesterol, all of which can raise "bad" (LDL) cholesterol, should be limited.
PRIMARILY SATURATED • Foods from animal sources (meat fat, butter, cheese, cream) • Coconut, palm, palm kernel oils	• Raises blood levels of "bad" (LDL) cholesterol	• Limit saturated fat.
PRIMARILY POLYUNSATURATED (PUFA) • Omega-3 fatty acids: herring, salmon, mackerel, lake trout, sardines, sword fish, nuts, flaxseed, rapeseed oil, soya bean oil, tofu • Omega-6: vegetable oils such as corn, soya bean, and safflower (abundant in the European diet)	• Reduces inflammation; influences blood clotting and blood vessel activity to improve blood flow	• Eat fish at least twice a week. • Substitute PUFA for saturated fat or trans fat when possible.
PRIMARILY MONOUNSATURATED (MUFA) Olive oil, rapeseed oil, sesame oil, avocados, almonds, chicken fat	• Raises blood levels of "good" (HDL) cholesterol	• Substitute MUFA for saturated fat or trans fats when possible.
DIETARY CHOLESTEROL Foods from animal sources (egg yolks, offal, cheese, fish roe, meat)	• A structural component of cell membranes and some hormones	• The body makes cholesterol, and some foods contain dietary cholesterol. British food labels list cholesterol values.
Trans fat Processed foods, purchased baked goods, margarine, and shortening	• Raises blood levels of "bad" (LDL) cholesterol	• British food labels will soon be listing trans fats.

VITAMINS

FAT-SOLUBLE VITAMINS AND FOOD SOURCES	FUNCTIONS	DAILY RECOMMENDED INTAKES FOR ADULTS*
Vitamin A Dairy foods, deep yellow-orange fruits and vegetables, dark green leafy vegetables, liver, fish, fortified milk, cheese, butter	• Promotes growth and healthy skin and hair • Helps build strong bones and teeth • Works as an antioxidant that may reduce the risk of some cancers and other diseases • Helps night vision • Increases immunity	700 mcg for women 900 mcg for men
Vitamin D Fortified milk, salmon, sardines, herring, butter, liver, fortified cereals, fortified margarine	• Builds bones and teeth • Enhances calcium and phosphorus absorption and regulates blood levels of these nutrients	5–10 mcg
Vitamin E Nuts and seeds, vegetable and seed oils (corn, soy, sunflower), whole-grain breads and cereals, dark green leafy vegetables, dried beans and peas	• Helps form red blood cells • Improves immunity • Prevents oxidation of LDL cholesterol • Works as an antioxidant that may reduce the risk of some cancers	15 mg
Vitamin K Dark green leafy vegetables, liver, carrots, asparagus, cauliflower, cabbage, wheat bran, wheat germ, eggs	• Needed for normal blood clotting • Promotes protein synthesis for bone, plasma, and organs	90 mcg for women 120 mcg for men

WATER-SOLUBLE VITAMINS

B vitamins Grain products, dried beans and peas, dark green leafy vegetables, dairy foods, meat, poultry, fish, eggs, offal, milk, brewer's yeast, wheat germ, seeds	• Help the body use carbohydrates (biotin, B_{12}, niacin, pantothenic acid) • Regulate metabolism of cells and energy production (niacin, pantothenic acid) • Keep the nerves and muscles healthy (thiamin) • Protect against spinal birth defects (folate) • Protect against heart disease (B_6, folate)	• B_6: 1.3–1.5 mg • B_{12}: 2.4 mcg (B_{12} is found only in animal-based food sources; vegetarians need supplements.) • Biotin: 30 mcg • Niacin: 14 mg niacin equivalents for women; 16 mg for men • Pantothenic acid: 5 mg • Riboflavin: 1.1 mg for women; 1.3 mg for men • Thiamin: 1.1 mg for women; 1.2 mg for men
Vitamin C Many fruits and vegetables, especially citrus fruits, broccoli, tomatoes, green peppers, melons, strawberries, potatoes, papayas	• Helps build body tissues • Fights infection and helps heal wounds • Helps body absorb iron and folate • Helps keep gums healthy • Works as an antioxidant	75 mg for women 90 mg for men

Sources: Institute of Medicine reports, 1999–2001

*mcg=micrograms; mg=milligrams

VITAMINS

MINERALS** AND FOOD SOURCES	FUNCTIONS	DAILY RECOMMENDED INTAKES FOR ADULTS*
Calcium Dairy foods (especially hard cheese, yoghurt, and milk), fortified juices, sardines and canned fish eaten with bones, shellfish, tofu (if processed with calcium), dark green leafy vegetables	• Helps build bones and teeth and keep them strong • Helps heart, muscles and nerves work properly	1,000–1,200 mg
Iron Meat, fish, shellfish, egg yolks, dark green leafy vegetables, dried beans and peas, grains, dried fruits	• Helps red blood cells carry oxygen • Component of enzymes • Strengthens immune system	18 mg for women 8 mg for men
Magnesium Nuts and seeds, whole-grain products, dark green leafy vegetables, dried beans and peas	• Helps build bones and teeth • Helps nerves and muscles work properly • Necessary for DNA and RNA • Necessary for carbohydrate metabolism	310–320 mg for women 400–420 mg for men
Phosphorus Seeds and nuts, meat, poultry, fish, dried beans and peas, dairy foods, whole-grain products, eggs, brewer's yeast	• Helps build strong bones and teeth • Has many metabolic functions • Helps body get energy from food	700 mg
Potassium Fruit, vegetables, dried beans and peas, meat, poultry, fish, dairy foods, whole grains	• Helps body maintain water and mineral balance • Regulates heartbeat and blood pressure	2,000 mg suggested; no official recommended intake
Selenium Seafood, chicken, offal, brown rice, whole-wheat bread, peanuts, onions	• Works as an antioxidant with vitamin E to protect cells from damage • Boosts immune function	55 mg
Zinc Oysters, meat, poultry, fish, soya beans, nuts, whole grains, wheat germ	• Helps body metabolise proteins, carbohydrates and alcohol • Helps wounds heal • Needed for growth, immune response and reproduction	8 mg for women 11 mg for men

** The following minerals are generally sufficient in the diet when the minerals listed above are present: chloride, chromium, copper, fluoride, iodine, manganese, molybdenum, sodium, and sulphur. For information on functions and food sources, consult a nutrition book.

Nutritional values

The recipes in this book have been analysed for significant nutrients to help you evaluate your diet and balance your meals throughout the day. Using these calculations, along with the other information in this book, you can create meals that have the optimum balance of nutrients. Having the following nutritional values at your fingertips will help you plan healthy meals.

Keep in mind that the calculations reflect nutrients per serving unless otherwise noted. Not included in the calculations are ingredients that are optional or added to taste, or those that are suggested as an alternative or substitution in the recipe, recipe note or variation. For recipes that yield a range of servings, the calculations are for the middle of that range. Many recipes call for a specific amount of salt and also suggest seasoning food to taste; however, if you are on a low-sodium diet, it is prudent to omit salt. If you have particular concerns about any nutrient needs, consult your doctor.

The numbers for all nutritional values have been rounded using the guidelines required for reporting nutrient levels in the "Nutrition Facts" panel on EU food labels.

The best way to acquire the nutrients your body needs is through food. However, a balanced multivitamin-mineral supplement or a fortified cereal that does not exceed 100 per cent of the daily need for any nutrient is a safe addition to your diet.

WHAT COUNTS AS A SERVING?	HOW MANY SERVINGS DO YOU NEED EACH DAY?		
	For a 1,600-calorie-per-day diet (children 2–6, sedentary women, some older adults)	For a 2,200-calorie-per-day diet (children over 6, teen girls, active women, sedentary men)	For a 2,800-calorie-per-day diet (teen boys, active men)
Fruit Group 1 medium whole fruit such as apple, orange, banana, or pear; 60–90 g (2–3 oz) chopped, cooked, or canned fruit; 90 g (3 oz) dried fruit; 180 ml (6 fl oz) fruit juice	2	3	4
Vegetable Group 30 g (1 oz) raw, leafy vegetables; 60–90 g (2–3 oz) other vegetables, cooked or raw; 180 ml (6 fl oz) vegetable juice	3	4	5
Bread, Cereal, Rice, and Pasta Group 1 slice of bread; 180 g (6 oz) ready-to-eat cereal; 80 g (2.5 oz) cooked cereal, rice, pasta	6	9	11

Adapted from USDA Dietary Guidelines (2005).

Purple & blue		CALORIES	PROTEIN/ GM	CARBS/ GM	TOT. FAT/ GM	SAT. FAT/ GM	CHOL/ MG	Fibre/ GM	SODIUM/ MG
p. 23	Blackberry crumble	517	7	79	22	11	34	8	30
p. 23	Raisin & cashew truffles (1 truffle)	70	1	8	4	2	0	1	10
p. 24	Lavender flans	183	8	25	6	3	142	0	94
p. 27	Blueberry cake with crunchy walnut topping	370	5	47	19	9	61	2	185
p. 30	Blackberry granita & cream parfait	257	1	50	7	4	24	1	17
p. 30	Sautéed plums with amaretto	197	2	39	3	2	8	2	25
p. 33	Prune compote with greek-style yoghurt	384	4	86	1	1	5	3	47
p. 34	Purple grape tart	252	5	40	8	5	114	1	52

Green		CALORIES	PROTEIN/ GM	CARBS/ GM	TOT. FAT/ GM	SAT. FAT/ GM	CHOL/ MG	Fibre/ GM	SODIUM/ MG
p. 41	Spiced apple cake	310	3	52	11	7	50	2	282
p. 41	Green tea punch	94	1	24	0	0	0	1	4
p. 42	Kiwi fruit sorbet	120	1	30	0	0	0	2	10
p. 42	Silky lime mousse	198	6	17	13	7	144	0	70
p. 45	Baked apples with caramel sauce	373	1	82	7	3	10	4	35
p. 45	Stuffed green pears	340	5	69	8	1	0	8	24
p. 48	Kiwi fruit tart with lime curd filling	490	6	55	29	17	191	2	66
p. 51	Minted green tea jellies with kiwi fruit	81	2	19	0	0	0	1	7

White & tan

		CALORIES	PROTEIN/ GM	CARBS/GM	TOT. FAT/ GM	SAT. FAT/ GM	CHOL/MG	Fibre/GM	SODIUM/ MG
p. 57	Ginger angel food cakes	230	4	54	0	0	0	0	114
p. 58	Caramelised bananas	250	2	44	9	6	23	2	14
p. 58	Sauternes-poached pears	413	1	66	0	0	0	5	15
p. 61	Crystallised-ginger gingerbread	223	3	41	5	3	50	1	148
p. 61	White nectarines with lychees & grapes	142	1	36	0	0	0	2	3
p. 64	Fresh dates with pistachio-mascarpone filling	367	6	54	17	8	36	6	27
p. 64	Brandied baked figs	195	1	37	0	0	0	4	2
p. 67	White peach crostatas	313	5	47	12	7	31	2	28
p. 67	Sweetcorn bread	498	9	75	18	2	62	4	519
p. 68	Streusel banana muffins	273	4	47	9	5	19	3	263

Yellow & orange

		CALORIES	PROTEIN/ GM	CARBS/GM	TOT. FAT/ GM	SAT. FAT/ GM	CHOL/MG	Fibre/GM	SODIUM/ MG
p. 75	Meyer lemon meringue ice cream	284	3	43	13	8	47	0	45
p. 75	Orange & sabayon gratin	265	3	42	5	3	113	4	11
p. 76	Papaya & mango tapioca	193	1	42	3	3	0	2	13
p. 76	Honey-glazed pineapple	143	1	38	0	0	0	2	2
p. 79	Roasted apricot & vanilla tart	258	4	40	9	6	23	2	28
p. 82	Carrot cupcakes with mascarpone icing	373	4	48	19	11	91	1	236
p. 85	Golden kiwi fruit pavlovas	350	4	58	13	8	47	2	75
p. 86	Lemon soufflés	112	1	28	0	0	0	0	19
p. 86	Sweet potato pie	310	5	39	16	9	106	2	180
p. 89	Golden fruit bowl with allspice syrup	90	1	23	0	0	0	2	6
p. 89	Golden cherry clafoutis	207	6	35	4	2	111	2	77

Red		CALORIES	PROTEIN/ GM	CARBS/GM	TOT. FAT/ GM	SAT. FAT/ GM	CHOL/MG	Fibre/GM	SODIUM/ MG
p. 95	Berry & ricotta trifles	522	12	88	14	7	140	3	182
p. 96	Plum cake	431	4	50	24	15	113	2	143
p. 96	Raspberry jellies	97	1	23	0	0	0	3	5
p. 99	Cherries flambéed in rum	298	2	51	6	4	13	2	10
p. 99	Rhubarb fool	319	2	31	22	14	82	1	25
p. 102	Brandied berry crêpes	182	4	27	5	3	62	3	96
p. 105	Pear & frangipane galettes	584	9	57	37	17	137	6	54
p. 105	Raspberries in red wine syrup	283	1	54	1	0	0	6	7
p. 106	Ruby grapefruit sorbet	156	2	38	0	0	0	0	17
p. 106	Redcurrant filo tarts	198	2	29	9	5	20	2	93

Brown		CALORIES	PROTEIN/ GM	CARBS/GM	TOT. FAT/ GM	SAT. FAT/ GM	CHOL/MG	Fibre/GM	SODIUM/ MG
p. 113	Prune panforte	210	4	31	9	1	0	3	3
p. 113	Brazil nut & almond torte	248	6	33	12	3	0	3	110
p. 114	Almond cake with kirsch syrup	220	6	33	7	1	115	1	75
p. 117	Hazelnut macaroons (1 macaroon)	41	1	7	1	0	0	0	14
p. 117	Real hot chocolate	335	11	39	20	11	20	3	100
p. 120	Chocolate-pumpkin cake	357	5	55	14	9	51	2	246
p. 120	Pistachio rice pudding	394	13	61	11	5	25	3	116
p. 123	Oatmeal pear crisp	394	5	65	15	9	36	7	88
p. 123	Bread pudding	247	8	30	11	5	122	2	147
p. 124	Walnut & date tart	288	5	42	13	4	66	2	56
p. 124	Polenta cake	313	4	28	20	5	40	2	78

Glossary

almonds: Like most nuts, almonds contain folate, riboflavin, and magnesium; they are also high in omega-3 fatty acids and vitamin E, an antioxidant that protects brain cells, promotes heart health, and lowers LDL (bad) cholesterol.

antioxidant: A substance that intercepts free radicals. Free radicals are unstable oxygen molecules created as our bodies process oxygen. Free radicals injure our other cells and promote damage and diseases ranging from cataracts and wrinkles to cancer and heart disease.

apples: The major portion of the apple's nutrition is in its skin, which contains the flavonoid quercetin, an antioxidant that fights viruses and allergies and is thought to be an anticarcinogenic. Apple flesh is an important source of pectin, a fibre that lowers cholesterol.

apricots: The apricot's colour is due to the pigments beta-carotene and lycopene, which promote eye health and heart health, lower the risk of some cancers, and strengthen the immune system. Apricots are also high in vitamin C, potassium, and fibre.

avocados: Technically a fruit, the avocado is high in fat, but most of it is monounsaturated, which helps to lower cholesterol. It also contains beta-sitosterol, a plant cholesterol that lowers cholesterol as well, and may prevent the growth of cancer cells. Avocados are high in vitamins and minerals, especially vitamins A, C, folate, B_6, and potassium.

bananas: Bananas are high in potassium, which helps to regulate blood pressure and may reduce arterial plaque formation and prevent strokes by lowering platelet activity and reducing blood clots. Bananas are also high in vitamins C and B_6 and contain a kind of fibre that may protect against colon cancer.

blackberries: Their dark purple colour is caused by anthocyanins, which help to lower the risk of some cancers and promote urinary tract health. Second only to blueberries in antioxidant content, they are also high in vitamin C, potassium, folate, and fibre.

blueberries: These native North American berries are so high in antioxidant and anti-inflammatory compounds that they are considered "brain food": they contain a range of anthocyanins, which are thought to help fight the damaging effects of ageing on the brain. Blueberries are available fresh, dried, and frozen. The European bilberry is a close relative.

Brazil nuts: Like all nuts, Brazil nuts are high in protein, fibre, minerals, and vitamin E, but their real claim to fame is their high proportion of selenium, a cancer-fighting antioxidant.

butter: An essential dairy product, butter is made by churning or agitating cream until the fats separate from the liquids and develop a semi-solid form. Butter is sold in two basic styles. More familiar is salted butter; for cooking and baking, however, most recipes call for unsalted butter. Unsalted butter lacks the additional salt that can interfere with the taste of the final recipe, and it is also likely to be fresher since salt often acts as a preservative, prolonging butter's shelf life. For the best quality, seek out butter that contains less moisture and more butterfat. If you cannot find unsalted butter, salted butter will work in most recipes; just taste and adjust the salt in the recipe as needed. To store unsalted butter that won't be used within a week or so, wrap it in freezer-weight plastic and freeze.

carrots: One carrot provides a whopping 330 per cent of the Daily Value of vitamin A, which is the source of its fame as a protector of vision. Carrots are also high in fibre and in bioflavonoids and carotenoids that lower the risk of some cancers, protect the heart, and boost immunity. Maroon and purple carrots contain antioxidants that promote healthy ageing.

cashews: Although they are higher in fat than many other nuts, cashews also contain magnesium and copper as well as the other usual beneficial compounds of nuts, such as protein and vitamin E.

cherries: Tart red and sweet, dark red cherries derive their colour from anthocyanin pigments and other antioxidants, which help to protect the heart and brain, lower the risk of some cancers, and are powerful anti-inflammatories. Both sweet and tart cherries also contain a terpenoid that prevents the growth of tumours.

chestnuts: Although far lower in fat than other nuts (8 per cent calories from fat, as opposed to the more than 75 per cent of most nuts), chestnuts are, like other nuts, high in protein, minerals, and cancer-fighting antioxidants in the form of flavonoids.

chocolate: Because it is a plant food, chocolate also contains phytochemicals, in the form of a group of antioxidants called catechins, also found in red wine. Dark chocolate is higher in these flavonoids (and lower in fat and sugar) than milk chocolate.

coffee: Like all plant foods, coffee contains beneficial phytochemicals. It is also high in the stimulant caffeine, to which some people are sensitive but which is being studied for its effects in countering Parkinson's disease and diabetes.

corn (maize): Sweetcorn is rich in vitamins, minerals, protein, and fibre. Yellow sweetcorn is given its colour by carotenoids that not only fight heart disease and cancer, but also protect against a type of damage to the eye called macular degeneration.

cranberries: High in both fibre and vitamin C, cranberries are excellent for preventing urinary tract infections due to their polyphenols. The anthocyanins that make cranberries red have antioxidant properties that protect the heart and may guard against cancer. Fresh, frozen, and dried cranberries, as well as cranberry juice, are all equally beneficial to health. European lingonberries are close relatives.

cream, double: When whipping cream, begin by chilling your equipment, including a metal bowl and the beaters, and use well-chilled double cream to yield the best results. Using an electric mixer on medium-high speed, beat cream until thick before adding sweetener, such as icing sugar, if using. "Soft peaks" means the cream forms peaks that gently slump to one side when the beaters are turned upright. Cream should not be whipped past the soft peak stage, or it will turn into butter. Use the cream immediately after whipping it.

currants: small dried Xanthe grapes. If they are unavailable, substitute raisins. Both currants and red grapes contain phenolic compounds, which may reduce the risk of heart disease and certain types of cancer.

dates: Occasionally available fresh in late summer and early autumn, dates are more commonly found smoked and dried, when their high sugar content increases greatly. They provide iron and protein.

figs: Whether eaten fresh (available in summer and early autumn) or dried, figs provide phosphorus, calcium, and iron. They also deliver different phytochemicals according to the colour of their skin – purple, tan, or green.

flambéing: Pouring spirits over a dish and igniting it is an essential step in many French dishes. To flambé safely, pour the alcohol into a pan away from the heat. Briefly place the pan on the heat to warm the alcohol, then remove it from the heat once more. Make sure any inflammable objects are moved away, and use a long kitchen match to flambé. Once the match is lit, hold it just above the alcohol to ignite the flames (you are lighting the fumes rising from the heated alcohol). The flame should burn out in 30 seconds. Keep a pot lid nearby to smother the flames if they don't subside within a minute.

flour, plain: Plain flour contains no raising agent. It is made from a mixture of refined soft and hard wheats. Strong, plain flour has a higher gluten content and is best for bread-making.

flour, soft-wheat: Low in protein and high in starch, soft-wheat flour is milled from soft strains of wheat and contains cornflour. It is fine-textured and has undergone a bleaching process that increases its ability to hold water and sugar. Cakes made with soft-wheat flour have a particularly soft, dense crumb.

ginger: Long prized in Chinese cuisine for its culinary and medicinal uses, ginger aids digestion, reduces nausea, and lowers cholesterol. It contains both antioxidant and anti-microbial compounds.

gooseberries: Available only briefly during the summer and early autumn, gooseberries are high in both vitamin C and fibre.

grapefruit: Half a grapefruit provides 70 per cent of the Daily Value of vitamin C. Pink or red grapefruit is high in vitamin A as well. All colours contain flavonoids that help to guard against cancer, while the red type also offers lycopene, another cancer-fighting antioxidant.

grapes: The dark purple Concord grape, native to the USA, is usually made into grape juice. It is high in antioxidants, making grape juice an important heart-healthy food. Red table grapes also promote heart health and immunity, and green grapes can help lower cancer risk and promote eye health.

guavas: Guavas are a rich source of vitamin C. One fruit contains 3 to 6 times more vitamin C than an orange, 10 to 30 times more than a banana, and about 10 times more than a papaya. Guavas are also a useful source of calcium, nicotinic acid, phosphorus, and soluble fibre. They are very good for the immune system and are beneficial in reducing cholesterol and protecting the heart.

hazelnuts: These flavourful nuts are especially high in vitamin E and contain a wide range of important minerals as well as dietary fibre.

herbs, green: Not only are fresh herbs rich in the phytochemicals that give them their colour and taste, they are important flavour enhancers for all vegetables and some fruits as well.

honey: Available in a range of flavours, from mild clover to intense chestnut, depending on the source of the pollen used by the bees to make this sweetener. The colour of a specific honey, from pale to dark, is a clue to the strength of its flavour. Raw, unfiltered honey contains minerals and also retains some pollen, but some individuals may have sensitivities to it in this form.

kiwi fruit: Extremely high in vitamin C (two kiwi fruits contain 240 per cent of Daily Value, almost twice as much as an orange), these fruits are also high in folate and potassium.

kumquats: These tiny oval orange citrus fruits are like backward oranges: the peel is sweet and the flesh is sour. Often candied or used sliced as an accent or whole or sliced as garnish, they are high in vitamin A, vitamin C, and potassium.

lavender: Long used as a relaxant, lavender is also a traditional Provençal culinary herb. It contains numerous phytochemicals, including perillyl alcohol, which apparently slows the growth of tumours and destroys cancer cells.

lemons: High in vitamin C, lemons are a flavour enhancer; add lemon juice to raw and cooked fruits and use it to replace salt at the table in vegetables and fish.

lime leaves, Kaffir: These aromatic leaves are used widely in Indian and South-east Asian cooking. Look for them in speciality food shops and Asian greengrocers.

limes: High in vitamin C, like all citrus fruits, lime juice also contains lutein, which benefits eye health. The Persian lime is widely available, while the yellowish green Key lime is usually found fresh in speciality food shops.

lychees: This fruit of Chinese origin is walnut-sized, with a bumpy red shell encasing white translucent pulp similar in texture to a grape. Lychees are very juicy, with a sweet flavour. Fresh lychees are available from May to July, and canned lychees are available year-round.

macadamia nuts: Macadamias are similar to other nuts in their fibre and beneficial omega-3 fatty acid content, and also contain phyto-sterols, which reduce LDL (bad) cholesterol and so promote heart health.

mangoes: This colourful orange tropical fruit is extremely high in vitamin A (160 per cent of Daily Value) and vitamin C (95 per cent of Daily Value). Mangoes also contain beta-carotene as well as quercetin, both of which are thought to fight cancer.

maple syrup: The early American colonists learned from local tribes of Native Americans how to tap maple trees for their sap and boil it down to make a sweetener. Grade A syrup, sometimes called Grade AA, is clear gold and has a mild, delicate flavour that complements waffles and pancakes. Grade B syrup is darker and has a richer, caramel-like flavour. Its stronger taste makes it more suitable for cooking.

melons: Higher in healthy nutrients than any other melon, the cantaloupe is also rich in vitamins A and C and potassium. It is heart-healthy and helps to lower the risk of cancer, thanks to its beta-carotene content. A wide variety of other orange-fleshed melons are also available. Green-fleshed melons such as Ogen contain cancer-fighting phytochemicals as well.

molasses: The dark residue of the sugar-making process, molasses comes in three forms: light, dark, and blackstrap. Although blackstrap molasses has been touted as highly nutritious, it is little more so than dark molasses, which is more palatable and similarly contains iron, calcium, and phosphorus. Black treacle has a similar nutritional value.

nectarines: Not a hybrid but a relative of the peach, the nectarine has the advantage of an edible skin that contains many of its phytochemicals. Yellow nectarines contain beta-carotene, while the pink-skinned, white-fleshed variety has its own group of beneficial compounds.

oats: Groats or pinhead oatmeal are whole grains that are steel-cut, to make porridge oats or oat flakes, or steamed and rolled into rolled oats. When the groats are cut into pieces and rolled thinner, they become quick-cooking oats. All of these forms retain their selenium and cholesterol-fighting nutrients, unlike instant oats. They are also high in vitamins B_1, B_6, and E.

oil, rapeseed: This bland-flavoured oil is pressed from rapeseed, a relative of the mustard plant. High in monounsaturated fat and neutral in flavour, it is a good choice for general cooking and baking.

oranges: Famed for their vitamin C content, oranges are also high in folate and potassium, as well as providing limonoids and flavonoids, both disease-fighting antioxidants.

papayas: With flesh ranging from yellow to orange to red, depending on their type, papayas are high in antioxidant carotenoids, which guard against certain cancers.

passion fruit: Named by a missionary after the Passion of Christ rather than for any earthly romantic feelings, this aromatic fruit has a tart, tropical flavour. Passion fruits are ripe when their inedible skins are wrinkled. Choose one that feels heavy for its size. The pulp and seeds are the parts you eat.

peaches: While its fuzzy skin is usually not eaten, the yellow or white flesh of the peach contains vitamins A and C and is available fresh, dried, frozen, and canned.

peanuts: Although they are not truly nuts, but pulses, peanuts are high in fat. They are a good source of protein, though they should be eaten in small amounts. Like most nuts, the fat they contain is largely monounsaturated.

pears: The beneficial pigments of pears are concentrated in their skin; as the skin is quite thin (except in the tan-skinned varieties), they can be eaten unpeeled, whether raw or cooked. The flesh contains vitamin A, as well as some phosphorus.

pecans: These nuts are rich in vitamin A and E, as well as heart-healthy sterols.

persimmons (kaki fruit, sharon fruit): Both the small, squat Fuyu or sharon fruit, and the larger, slightly pointed Hachiya must be eaten fully ripe, or they will taste "furry" due to their high tannic acid content. They are rich in beta-carotene and vitamin C.

phytochemicals: These natural compounds found in plants impart colours, flavours, and scents to the plant to attract insects and animals that help the plant reproduce or ward off predators. Some phytochemicals help protect against environmental dangers such as radiation from the sun or viruses and other diseases. When these compounds are ingested by humans or animals, they continue to carry out these same functions, preventing damage to cells and diseases and boosting the immune system.

pineapples: The pineapple's sweet, juicy flesh provides manganese, vitamins A and C, and bromelain, an anti-inflammatory enzyme that also acts as a digestive aid.

pine nuts: Delicate, buttery pine nuts contain both iron and thiamin. Used in both Mexican and Italian cooking, they can also be a flavourful garnish for salads and cooked foods.

pistachios: The sweet, pale green flesh of this nut contains potassium and vitamin B$_6$. Look for unsalted shelled pistachios in bulk in healthfood shops. Their papery skins can be removed after toasting by rubbing them in a towel, as for hazelnuts.

plums: The edible skin of the plum, which comes in a variety of colours, contains most of its phytochemicals, though the yellow, purple, green, or red flesh also has beneficial compounds. A good source of vitamin C, plums are one of the most healthy fruits.

poaching: Cooking in liquid at a temperature just below the boiling point, poaching is a gentle method that works well for delicate foods such as fruit. The poaching liquid is sometimes reduced to make a sauce. Heating fruit along with the poaching liquid, rather than adding it to an already-simmering mixture, causes the flavour of the fruit to infuse the syrupy liquid. Once the liquid comes to a boil, reduce the heat as needed to maintain a gentle simmer, with slow bubbles breaking the surface.

polenta: Although polenta is sometimes made from other dried grains or white sweetcorn, usually it is coarsely or finely ground yellow cornmeal. Stone-ground cornmeal is higher in quality but also perishable; store it in an airtight container in the refrigerator.

pomegranates: The fleshy seeds of this fruit are high in vitamin C, potassium, and heart-healthy anthocyanins. The fruit is in season during the autumn months, while pomegranate juice is available year-round in healthfood stores and some supermarkets.

prunes: These dried prune plums, now also called dried plums, are rich in vitamin A, potassium, and fibre. They are higher in antioxidants than any other fruit or vegetable, making them a top anti-ageing food.

pumpkins: The flesh of the pumpkin is nutrient-rich with vitamin A and carotenoids, specifically the cancer-fighters alpha- and beta-carotene and lutein. Choose pumpkins that are unblemished and heavy for their size.

pumpkin seeds: High in fibre, protein, and various minerals, pumpkin seeds also contain beta-sitosterol, which lowers cholesterol and slows the growth of abnormal cells. Clean and toast your own, or buy them in health food shops.

quinces: Although it bears a resemblance to an apple or pear, the quince is not a fruit that can be eaten raw. The uncooked flesh is very hard, dry and astringent in taste. However, when slowly cooked, a quince will develop an aromatic scent and delightfully mellow flavour. Raw quince may be pale green like a Granny Smith apple or yellow like a Golden Delicious, but takes on a pink to ruby hue as it cooks and red phytochemicals develop in its flesh.

raisins: Antioxidant rich, raisins are also high in vitamins, minerals, and fibre. Both raisins and sultanas start as green grapes, but sultanas are treated with sulphur dioxide to prevent oxidation.

raspberries: Red raspberries contain more fibre than most other fruits; they are also high in vitamin C and folate, and extremely high in cancer-fighting antioxidants. Golden

raspberries are less common, but they contain heart- and eye-health bioflavonoids. Although fresh raspberries are fragile, frozen unsweetened raspberries retain their flavour and are available year-round.

redcurrants: These are the red variety of the currant, a bush that is native to western Europe. Redcurrants are very rich in vitamin C: 112 g will provide 77 per cent of Daily Value. They also contain calcium, iron, potassium, and manganese. Whitecurrants are merely a colourless variety of redcurrant, but blackcurrants, though closely related and equally nutritious, are a different species.

rhubarb: These tart red stalks are one of the first signs of spring when they appear in the market. High in vitamin A and beneficial phytochemicals, rhubarb helps to protect the heart, boost immunity, and lower the risk of some cancers.

sesame seeds: Flat and minute, sesame seeds come in several colours, but are most commonly a light ivory. They are rich in minerals such as manganese, copper, and calcium and also contain cholesterol-lowering lignans. Because they have a high oil content, they should be kept refrigerated. Toasting brings out their nutty flavour.

spring onions: Like all onions, spring onions contain organosulphur compounds, which are thought to protect the heart and improve the ratio of good to bad cholesterol.

strawberries: Rich in antioxidant content, partly due to their anthocyanin pigments, strawberries are also extremely high in vitamin C. Because of these compounds, as well as their phenolic acids, these berries are thought to be important cancer-fighters.

sugar: The most common sugar is granulated white sugar, which has been extracted from sugar cane or sugar beet and refined by boiling, centrifuging, chemical treatment, and straining. For baking recipes, buy only sugar that is labelled cane sugar; beet sugar may have an unpredictable effect. Most sugars marketed as "raw" are actually partially refined. Turbinado, a common raw sugar, has light brown, coarse crystals. Muscovado and Barbados are also varieties of raw sugar.

sugar, brown: Rich in flavour, brown sugar is granulated sugar coloured with molasses. It has a soft, moist texture and comes in mild-flavoured light brown and strongly flavoured dark brown varieties.

sugar, caster: When finely ground, granulated sugar becomes caster or castor sugar. Because it dissolves rapidly, this sugar is preferred for delicate mixtures such as beaten egg whites and cold recipes such as mixed drinks. It is ideal for making candied citrus peel because the sugar will coat the peel evenly. To make your own, process granulated sugar in a food processor until finer granules form.

sunflower seeds: Nutty-flavoured sunflower seeds are rich in iron and protein and may be added to breads and other baked goods or used as a nutritious garnish to add texture to many dishes.

sweet potatoes: The most commonly available of these root vegetables are a pale yellow variety and a dark orange one. White sweet potatoes with a purple tinge are sometimes available. All are high in fibre, vitamins A and C, and a host of other vitamins and minerals, as well as more beta-carotene than any other vegetable.

tea, green: Green tea is made from steamed and dried tea leaves that – unlike the leaves for black tea – have not been fermented. Both kinds of tea are rich in phytochemicals and appear to fight cardiovascular disease, including stroke, and cancers of the gastro-intestinal tract and, surprisingly, skin. And green tea's delicate flavour translates to a light, refreshing dessert. Though convenient, tea bags do not make the best tea, as the leaves are not able to circulate. For better flavour, seek out high-quality loose tea or powder sold at tea shops or speciality food shops.

walnuts: With the same high levels of protein and vitamin E as most other nuts, walnuts are also especially rich in omega-3 oils, as well as ellagic acid, which helps to lower the risk of cancer.

water-melon: Despite its high water content, this melon provides vitamins A and C, along with the anthocyanins that give it its bright red colour. Yellow-fleshed watermelons are sometimes available and they contain different nutrients.

wheat, whole: The bran in whole wheat contains selenium and other minerals, as well as vitamin E. Whole wheat is also an important source of fibre, which is thought to help lower the risk of strokes and heart disease. As with all whole grains, all forms of whole wheat, from wheat germ to flour, should be kept refrigerated.

wine: The colours of red and rosé wines are due to the skins of the purple grapes used to make the wines; because of the way the skins are used in red wine production, red wine contains more beneficial antioxidants called phenolics than grape juice. These phytochemicals are believed to contribute to heart health. Additionally, moderate consumption of alcohol such as wine has been shown to lower the level of bad cholesterol and increase the level of good cholesterol.

Bibliography

The resources below were used in the creation of this book, and are recommended for further reading on the subject of colourful plant foods:

BOOKS

Gollman, Barbara, and Kim Pierce. *The Phytopia Cookbook*. Dallas, Tex.: Phytopia, Inc., 1998.

Green, Eliza. *Field Guide to Produce*. Philadelphia: Quirk Books, 2004.

Heber, David, M.D., Ph.D. *What Color Is Your Diet?* New York: Harper Collins, 2001.

Hess, Mary Abbott, L.H.D., M.S., R.D., F.A.D.A; Dana Jacobi; and Marie Simmons. *Williams-Sonoma Essentials of Healthful Cooking*. Menlo Park, Calif.: Oxmoor House, 2003.

Joseph, James A., Ph.D.; Daniel A. Nadeau, M.D.; and Anne Underwood. *The Color Code*. New York: Hyperion, 2002.

Pivonka, Elizabeth, R.D., Ph.D., and Barbara Berry, M.S., R.D. *5 a Day: The Better Health Cookbook*. New York: Rodale, 2002.

Tantillo, Tony, and Sam Gugino. *Eat Fresh, Stay Healthy*. New York: Macmillan General Reference, 1997.

WEBSITES

Cancer Research UK – Healthy Living: http://info.cancerresearchuk.org/healthyliving

Produce for Better Health Foundation: http://www.5aday.org

United States Department of Agriculture: http://www.usda.gov

University of California, Berkeley, School of Public Health Wellness Letter: http://www.wellnessletter.com

Index

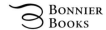

BONNIER BOOKS

Appledram Barns
Birdham Road
Chichester, West Sussex
PO20 7EQ

WELDON OWEN INC.

Chief Executive Officer John Owen

President and Chief Operating Officer Terry Newell

Chief Financial Officer Christine E. Munson

Vice President International Sales Stuart Laurence

Vice President and Creative Director Gaye Allen

Vice President and Publisher Hannah Rahill

Associate Publisher Sarah Putman Clegg

Editor Emily Miller

Editorial Assistant Juli Vendzules

Photo Director and Senior Designer Marisa Kwek

Production Director Chris Hemesath

Colour Manager Teri Bell

Production and Reprint Coordinator Todd Rechner

NEW HEALTHY KITCHEN *DESSERTS*

Previously published as Williams-Sonoma New Healthy Kitchen Desserts

Conceived and produced by Weldon Owen Inc.
814 Montgomery Street, San Francisco, CA 94133, USA
Telephone: 415 291 0100   Fax: 415 291 8841

In collaboration with Williams-Sonoma, Inc.
3250 Van Ness Avenue, San Francisco, CA 94109

A WELDON OWEN PRODUCTION
Copyright © 2006 by Weldon Owen Inc. and Williams-Sonoma Inc.

Set in Vectora

Colour separations by Mission Productions Limited
Printed and bound in China by Midas Printing Limited

First printed in 2006.

10 9 8 7 6 5 4 3 2 1

Library of Congress Cataloging-in-Publication data is available.

ISBN: 978-1-905825-00-4

ACKNOWLEDGMENTS

Weldon Owen wishes to thank the following people for their generous support in producing this book: **Copy Editor** Carolyn Miller; **Consulting Editor** Judith Dunham; **Proofreaders** Desne Ahlers, Carrie Bradley, Leslie Evans, and Kate Washington; **Indexer** Ken DellaPenta; **Translator** Josephine Bacon; **Production Editor** Joan Olson; Adrienne Aquino; Karen Brux; Carol Hacker; Jackie Mills; Marianne Mitten; Shadin Saah; and Richard Yu

Photographer Dan Goldberg

Photographer's Assistant Julie Caine

Food Stylist Jen Straus

Assistant Food Stylist Max La Rivière-Hedrick

The images on the following pages were created by this photo team:
8–9; 18 *top left;* 21; 22; 25; 26; 28 *bottom;* 29; 31; 36; 39; 40; 43; 46 *top;* 47; 49; 52 *top left, bottom left, bottom right;* 62; 63 *bottom;* 69; 70 *top left;* 73; 77; 80; 81 *top;* 83; 84; 87; 90 *bottom left, bottom right;* 93; 97; 98; 101 *top;* 104; 107; 108 *top left, bottom right;* 112; 118 *top;* 121.

Photographer Ben Dearnley

Food and Prop Stylist Julz Beresford

Assistant Food Stylist Jess Sly

The images on the following pages were created by this photo team:
18 *top right, bottom left, bottom right;* 28 *top;* 32; 35; 44; 46 *bottom;* 50; 52 *top right;* 55; 56; 59; 60; 63 *top;* 65; 66; 70 *top right, bottom left, bottom right;* 74; 78; 81 *bottom;* 88; 90 *top left, top right;* 94; 100; 101 *bottom;* 103; 108 *top right, bottom left;* 111; 115; 116; 118 *bottom;* 119; 122; 125.